FIRST CITIES

For Mary

SMITHSONIAN
EXPLORING THE ANCIENT WORLD
JEREMY A. SABLOFF, Editor

FIRST CITIES

By ANTHONY P. ANDREWS

St. Remy Press • Montreal

Smithsonian Books • Washington, D.C.

EXPLORING THE ANCIENT WORLD
was produced by
ST. REMY PRESS

Publisher	Kenneth Winchester
President	Pierre Léveillé
Managing Editor	Carolyn Jackson
Managing Art Director	Diane Denoncourt
Production Manager	Michelle Turbide
Picture Editor	Christopher Jackson
Administrator	Natalie Watanabe

Staff for *FIRST CITIES*

Editor	Alfred LeMaitre
Art Director	Philippe Arnoldi
Assistant Editor	Jennifer Meltzer
Picture Researcher	Geneviève Monette
Systems Coordinator	Eric Beaulieu
Secretary	Lorraine Doré
Administrative Assistant	Dominique Gagné
Indexer	Christine Jacobs
Proofreader/Researcher	Olga Dzatko

THE SMITHSONIAN INSTITUTION

Secretary	I. Michael Heyman
Assistant Secretary for External Affairs	Thomas E. Lovejoy
Acting Director, Smithsonian Institution Press	Daniel Goodwin

SMITHSONIAN BOOKS

Editor-in-Chief	Patricia Gallagher
Senior Editor	Alexis Doster III
Editors	Amy Donovan
	Joe Goodwin
Associate Editors	Bryan D. Kennedy
	Sonia Reece
Assistant Editor	Robert Lockhart
Senior Picture Editor	Frances C. Rowsell
Picture Editors	Carrie F. Bruns
	R. Jenny Takacs
Production Editor	Patricia Upchurch
Business Manager	Stephen J. Bergstrom
Marketing Manager	Susan E. Romatowski

FRONT COVER PHOTO: *The Street of the Dead, seen from the Pyramid of the Moon, was the major artery of Teotihuacán.*

BACK COVER PHOTO: *The excavation of the Royal Cemetery at Ur brought to light this wooden he-goat covered with gold, silver, and lapis lazuli.*

Library of Congress Cataloging-in-Publication Data
Andrews, Anthony P.
   First Cities / by Anthony P. Andrews
      p. cm. — (Exploring the ancient world)
   Includes bibliographical references (p.) and index.
   ISBN 0-89599-043-1
   1. Cities and towns, Ancient. 2. Urbanization
   I. Title. II. Series.
   HT114.A54   1994
   307.76—dc20   94-39479
                                    CIP

Manufactured and printed in Canada.
First Edition

10 9 8 7 6 5 4 3 2 1

CONTENTS

EDITOR'S FOREWORD

It does not take much insight to realize that the urbanization of our planet is one of the most important phenomena of the 20th century. Moreover, as many writers have indicated, if current trends continue, urbanization will certainly become even more significant in the next century. The problems with modern cities are legion, with overcrowding, poverty, pollution, traffic, and violent crime just a few of the critical areas we read about every day in the newspapers. Yet despite all of the well-publicized, negative aspects of urban life, people still flock to cities around the globe, and cities continue to grow inexorably in size. How can archaeological research be relevant to these modern trends? Although archaeology obviously cannot solve today's urban ills, it can provide an historical context for planners who need to understand why and how cities first emerged and the nature of their growth over thousands of years. Perhaps a better understanding of the successes and failures of past cities will help provide people today with new ideas about how to tackle the current urban crisis.

Thus, Professor Anthony Andrews' fascinating introduction to the cities of the pre-industrial world should be of interest to a wide variety of readers, from archaeology buffs to those concerned with the urban phenomenon. In a scholarly tour de force, Professor Andrews synthesizes archaeological and historical data on early cities from all over the world and presents this highly diverse information in clear and readable form. He discusses the links between cities and states and then proceeds to describe the rise of urban complexity in the ancient world. In a series of illuminating chapters, he reviews the latest archaeological evidence from Mesopotamia, Egypt, the Indus, and China in the Old World and the Mexican highlands, the Maya lowlands, and the Andes in the New World. The cultural situation prior to the rise of the first cities is summarized in each case, and the factors leading to urban development are noted. Professor Andrews then discusses the nature of the early cities and how they functioned.

Dr. Anthony P. Andrews is highly qualified to write this book. He is a Professor of Anthropology and Chair of the Division of Social Sciences at New College, the University of South Florida. Professor Andrews, who received his doctorate from the University of Arizona, is an expert on Maya archaeology and has extensive field experience in the northern Maya lowlands.

He is the author of *Maya Salt Production and Trade* (1983), several archaeological monographs, and numerous scholarly articles.

If Professor Andrews had been writing a similar book even a decade ago, his difficult task would have been considerably tougher. Significant archaeological research in recent years—particularly studies of urban settlements—has cast important new light on the rise of cities in many parts of the globe. Until recently, in fact, some scholars believed that neither the ancient Egyptian nor Maya civilizations had cities at all. However, as archaeologists have begun to consistently look beyond the great temples and palaces to uncover and map the houses and workplaces of the full range of past complex societies, a new picture of the full extent of urbanism, not only in Egypt and the Maya area but throughout the ancient world, has begun to emerge. As Professor Andrews clearly shows, if archaeologists are to understand how early cities developed and how they were supported, the humble peasant or serf or artisan deserves as much scholarly attention as the wealthy and powerful ruling elite. The results of new settlement pattern studies from Mesopotamia to the Andes are pointed out by Professor Andrews, who carefully notes their implications for expanding our understanding of ancient urbanism.

Archaeological studies of early pre-industrial cities have led to many new insights into the rise of these urban centers. Such studies represent one of the most exciting intellectual areas in modern archaeological research. In the pages that follow, Professor Andrews shares a number of these insights with the reader, who will learn about the key factors in the rise of cities and gain a richer appreciation for the similarities and differences between the Old and New Worlds in the emergence of the first cities.

Jeremy A. Sabloff
University of Pennsylvania
Museum of Archaeology and Anthropology

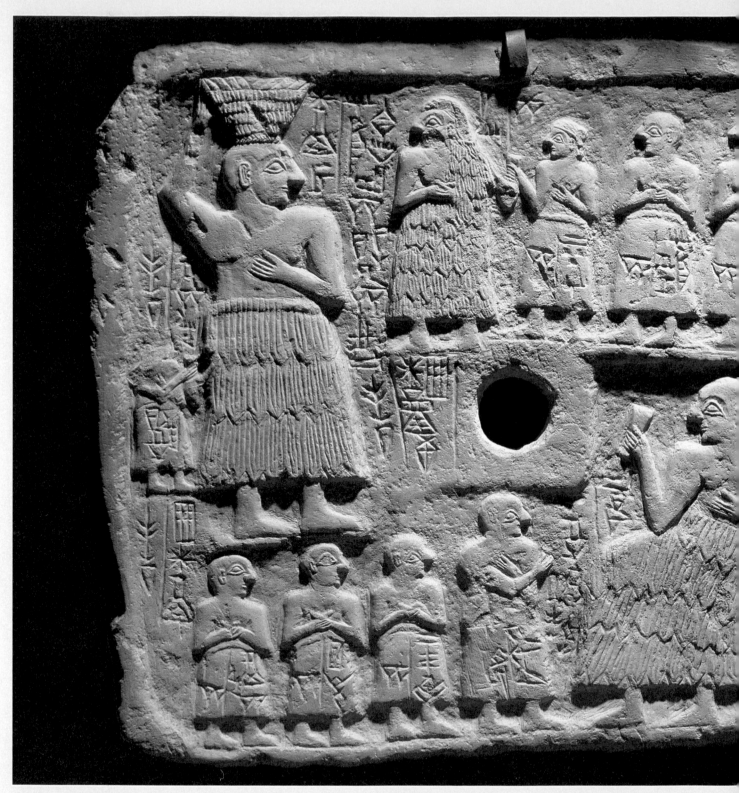

Carved in relief, this wall plaque from Telloh, in ancient Sumeria, depicts the great King Ur-Nanshe of Lagash carrying a basket of bricks to be used section, he toasts its completion. The hole in the plaque's center is thought to have been made for a peg that affixed the plaque to a wall.

in the construction of a temple. In the lower

1

CITIES, STATES, AND CIVILIZATION

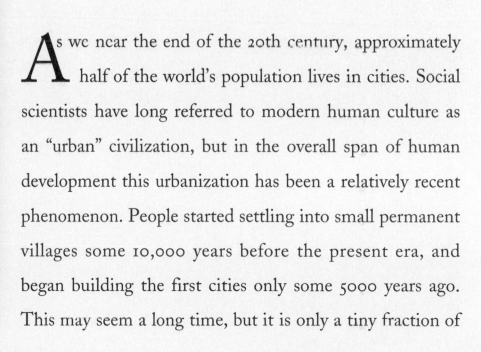

As we near the end of the 20th century, approximately half of the world's population lives in cities. Social scientists have long referred to modern human culture as an "urban" civilization, but in the overall span of human development this urbanization has been a relatively recent phenomenon. People started settling into small permanent villages some 10,000 years before the present era, and began building the first cities only some 5000 years ago. This may seem a long time, but it is only a tiny fraction of

Gordon R. Willey, seen here in 1946, is today considered the dean of New World archaeology. In the early 1940s, Willey pioneered the study of ancient settlement patterns, an approach that marked a turning point in the study of early cities.

the lifespan of our species. Prior to the appearance of the first villages, human beings led a nomadic, hunting-and-gathering way of life, and did so quite successfully for more than two million years. The transition to an urban way of life has occupied less than one percent of the time of our existence on Earth.

Given the relatively short time we have lived in cities, it is not surprising to find that we are still in the process of adapting to this new way of life. Daily newspaper headlines and myriad scholarly studies indicate that urban life is beset with problems: inadequate infrastructure, inefficient (and sometimes corrupt) management, overcrowding, pollution, poverty, crime, and violence. Yet people around the world continue to flock to cities, for a variety of reasons. The primary pull is economic, but the urban lifestyle and its amenities are powerful magnets as well. Most of those who eventually choose to leave the city don't really go that far away—they generally move to the suburbs or nearby towns, where they still enjoy access to urban jobs and the benefits of city life. Even people living in small towns often cannot avoid becoming urban, as metropolitan areas and "corridors" spread outward, swallowing ever larger parts of the countryside. In short, the trend toward urban living appears to be an irreversible process. It is estimated that by the year 2050, less than 25 percent of the world's population will still be living in rural areas.

To better understand this process—one that is central to the evolution of human culture—archaeologists, for more than a century, have been exploring and excavating the earliest villages, towns, and cities around the world. This research has many objectives, but central among them are determining when and where cities first appeared and identifying the processes that led to their emergence. This work has given rise to a sophisticated vision of the first cities. Much remains to be done, but we now have a reasonably good idea where and when the first cities appeared, how they functioned, and how their inhabitants lived. We have also made tentative attempts to explain why many of those cities arose.

This book describes the earliest cities in those parts of the world where state-level societies first appeared, namely Mesopotamia, Egypt, the Indus region, China, Mesoamerica, and the Andes. It does not cover the later cities of many areas, such as those of the Late Bronze and Iron ages of the Old World or those that arose in the later stages of pre-Hispanic development of the New World, such as the Postclassic Maya, Toltecs, or Aztecs, or the Chimú and Inca cities of the Andes.

THE ARCHAEOLOGY OF EARLY URBANISM

The archaeology of urbanism has come a long way since the exploration of ancient cities began in the 19th century. In the olden days, archaeologists were attracted to the highly visible monumental features of cities, and early excavations tended to focus on large civic-religious structures, palaces, massive sculptures, paintings, and the elaborate tombs of the rich and famous.

The desire to find exotic artifacts and mummies for museum displays was an early concern of many of these excavations. This tradition of "palace archaeology" had its shortcomings, the main one being that we developed a lopsided view of ancient cities, one that focused almost exclusively on the elite sectors of society and ignored the remains of the larger settlement and its less affluent population. Ironically, it was this larger population—the workers, artisans, merchants, and other specialists—that drove the economy and made the city what it was.

The development of settlement-pattern research, pioneered by archaeologist Gordon Willey in the 1940s, shifted the focus toward a "holistic" approach to ancient settlements. Aided by technological advances, such as aerial photography and more precise dating techniques, this new approach began with detailed surveys of entire communities, and produced a much sharper vision of the growth of urban settlements, their internal organization and diversity, and their ties to the rural hinterland. Excavations also began to focus on individual households, specialized buildings, and workshops, leading to the identification of different sectors of the population, their occupations, and, in some instances, their ethnic affiliations. An example of the latter has been the identification of a *barrio* (district) for foreign Oaxacan merchants in the central Mexican city of Teotihuacán. Studies such as these have yielded considerable data on the social, economic, political, and ideological organization of early urban life, as well as the environmental contexts of ancient cities.

One of the first problems that archaeologists encountered in their study of early cities was how to arrive at a formal definition of a true urban center. Part of the problem lay in the widespread and uncritical use of the terms "city" and "civilization" in the popular literature, which continues to this day. It is not unusual, for example, to run across an article touting the discovery of a lost "civilization" in the jungles of South America, in which the writer describes the ruins of a small settlement in a remote part of the Andes, which turns out to have been an outpost of the Inca Empire. In the same vein, popular writers use the term "ancient city" to describe almost any abandoned settlement that has a few ruined buildings; witness the widespread references to the "ancient cities" of the prehistoric American Southwest, which are not urban settlements by any definition.

The archaeologist V. Gordon Childe first addressed this problem in 1950 by selecting a series of characteristics that he felt defined a truly urban society. Archaeologist Charles Redman and others have summarized these as follows:

1) A large and dense population
2) Full-time specialization of labor; large-scale craft production and specialization
3) A class-structured society, including a ruling class of religious, political, and military functionaries

Australian-born V. Gordon Childe, shown here in 1927, was the first archaeologist to establish criteria for defining a truly urban society. These criteria included a class structure, a system of taxation, an organized labor force, long-distance trade, and most important, a state organization that included a bureaucracy and a military apparatus.

4) A system of taxation or tribute allowing for a centrally controlled concentration of surplus
5) A state-level organization, with a bureaucracy and military apparatus, and a defined political domain with territorial boundaries
6) Monumental public works—collective enterprises such as temples, palaces, storehouses, and irrigation systems
7) Standardized monumental artwork, reflecting a shared aesthetic and symbolic system
8) Long-distance trade
9) Writing
10) Exact, predictive scientific knowledge (basic arithmetic, geometry, and astronomy).

Most ancient urban societies do in fact exhibit all of these characteristics, with the exception of writing, which was lacking in the earliest urban cultures of central Mexico (Teotihuacán) and the Andes. However, systems of recording were later developed in both of those areas: the Aztecs had glyphs for numbers, places, and objects; the Inca a numerical counting device, known as a *quipu*, made up of hundreds of knotted strings tied to a ring.

Just how large must a community be to legitimately qualify as a city? There is no absolute answer to this question; even modern city planners cannot agree on a formal quantitative definition of a city. In dealing with early urban centers, many archaeologists would accept a minimum population of 5000 people, though some would prefer a figure of 10,000. And, of course, the population must be densely concentrated. There is more latitude in defining density, as many primitive cities had extensive (widely dispersed) rather than intensive (dense and closely packed) settlement patterns. The earliest cities had ample room to grow, and their inhabitants lived in single-story—in some instances two-story—residences, and often included large open spaces and garden plots within the city. Once again, a minimal figure of 1300 people per square mile (500 per square kilometer) would satisfy many archaeologists, though some might argue for higher densities.

A basic feature that V. Gordon Childe and later scholars felt was critical to a definition of urbanism was the existence of a state level of organization. Such an organization is central to the complex infrastructure of urban life, and the two go hand-in-hand. Thus when we speak of the rise of the first cities, we also mean the emergence of the state. Simply put, pre-state-level societies, such as tribes and chiefdoms, do not have true cities. Within this context, then, it is possible to provide a more formal definition of that oft-misused term, "civilization"; most scholars would likely accept the notion that a true civilization is one with a complex level of cultural development, which includes fully formed urbanism and a state level of organization. Still, some scholars use the term "civilization" to describe less complex societies, such as those of the Olmec, Chavín, or Preclassic Maya, which had simple regional polities governed by complex communities that were not fully urban.

A clay map highlights the all-important role of irrigation in ancient Mesopotamia, depicting the vein-like pattern of canals that were required to maintain crop growth in the fields of the city of Nippur.

Defining the urban nature of an ancient settlement is not the ultimate objective of archaeological research. A more important objective is to trace the growth of the city, as well as to attempt to explain the processes that led to the emergence of an urban way of life. This is the ultimate challenge, as we can only arrive at a better understanding of the urban phenomenon by elucidating the causes of its development.

THE RISE OF CITIES AND STATES
In writing about the rise of the cities of the ancient Near East, V. Gordon Childe favored an economic explanation for the emergence of urban life.

The early inhabitants of the Andes adapted irrigation to their high-altitude environment. While the wide floors of the region's highland valleys, such as this one, are rich in arable land, the steep slopes of the valleys are not naturally suited to cultivation. However, by redirecting runoff from the melting snows and by terracing the hillsides, Andean farmers have for centuries been able to grow crops on seemingly unworkable land.

Specifically, he proposed that surpluses of food from intensive agriculture made possible by the use of irrigation systems, coupled with craft specialization and trade, were the driving forces behind the increasing social complexity that gave rise to urban settlements, states, and civilizations. Since then, various archaeologists and historians, including Karl Wittfogel, Robert Adams, William Rathje, Charles Redman, Colin Renfrew, and Elman Service have advanced theories proposing different prime movers for the rise of cities and state-level societies around the world. These include population growth, craft specialization and trade, agricultural intensification (irrigation systems), and warfare and conquest.

Individually, none of these factors can generate social complexity. Still, their interaction can provide the major driving force in the rise of complex political systems. A large population is a basic characteristic of urban communities, and population growth can fuel increasing social and economic complexity, intensification of agriculture, and competition over land and resources. Several scholars have further advanced Childe's argument that craft specialization and trade are powerful forces behind the emergence of a diversified economy and the emergence of economic elites. In a scenario originally proposed by Wittfogel and applied to Late Dynastic China, the development of irrigation systems may have played a factor in the rise of a managerial elite, with resulting growth in surpluses managed by that elite, and increased social stratification. Warfare and conquest, whether generated by overpopulation, the desire to acquire new lands and resources (such as one's neighbor's irrigation system), or competition for trade routes, can lead to the creation of a powerful military class, which in turn can be a pivotal building block of complex political systems.

The environment also has influenced the rise of many early cities and civilizations. The environmental setting of a number of early civilizations, while admittedly a passive factor, often provided ample opportunities for challenges to demographic and economic growth. The development of early urban civilizations along river basins offers a case in point: rivers provide water for irrigation systems and transport for commerce. In a similar vein, access to a varied mosaic of ecological niches, in which climate, vegetation, and rainfall change dramatically with every few thousand feet of altitude, and to the rich resources found therein, played a critical role in the growth of social complexity in the Andes.

Ideology looms large in the emergence of every one of the world's early civilizations. Religion is a powerful cohesive social force, and provides a shared set of beliefs, values, and social identity in many cultures. Religious monuments are a prominent feature of all early cities, and clearly reflect the preeminent role that centralized religion played in the organization of the city and in the daily life of its people. This is also evident in the development of art, which served as a medium for expressing commonly held ideological themes. The manipulation of these themes by the elites was a powerful instrument in the consolidation of early states, whose political organization invariably had a strong theocratic component.

The debates over the various causes behind the rise of urbanism and statehood have been driven in part by a search for common denominators and for a universal model that would account for this social phenomenon. However, as research progresses, there is a growing consensus that while most regions shared many of the prime ingredients, the mix of factors that led to social complexity varies from region to region. As we shall see in the following pages, each region is unique in its own right. This is not surprising, given the differing environments and the cultural diversity found throughout the world today: one would expect to find differences between the evolution of the societies of the Mesopotamian desert and that of the peoples of the tropical Maya lowlands. Still, the basic question persists: despite distinctive regional variations, does the emergence of complex society have certain universal patterns?

In the pages that follow we focus on the independent growth and development of urban traditions in those parts of the world where cities first appeared. It is not our purpose merely to describe these early cities, interesting as they may be in their own right. Rather, we will focus on the processes that led to the rise of urban traditions, and attempt to define the major factors that led to the establishment of the earliest cities. Along the way, we shall look at the distinctive features that made each regional urban tradition unique, while at the same time exploring those characteristics that were shared by some, or all, of the earliest urban societies around the world.

The Tigris and Euphrates rivers converge in southeastern Iraq to form vast marshes before emptying into the Persian Gulf. The rivers nourished ting the growth of the earliest farming communities, and feeding the major irrigation projects undertaken by the region's emerging states.

THE NEAR EAST: CRADLE OF CIVILIZATION

The Near East, where the continents of Africa, Asia, and Europe come together, has long been known as the "cradle of civilization". Home of the biblical Garden of Eden, where people first planted crops and settled into villages, it is also the region where the earliest cities in the world appeared. This oldest of urban traditions arose out of a long development of villages and towns, going back to 9000 B.C. The first true cities, the city-states of ancient Sumer, appeared 5000 years ago in the lower drainage of

the civilizations of ancient Mesopotamia, permit-

the Tigris and Euphrates rivers of southern Mesopotamia, in what today is Iraq.

The Near East offered a favorable setting for the first farmers and city-dwellers. The geographic and ecological configuration of the region is often described as a "Fertile Crescent". The crescent is defined by a semicircle of foothills, mountains, and intermontane valleys that originate in the hills of the southern Levant, continue up into Lebanon, Syria, and the Taurus Mountains of eastern Turkey, and then curve downward along the Zagros mountain chain that runs from Iraqi Kurdistan into western Iran.

Several distinct ecological regions can be defined in the Fertile Crescent and its surrounding areas. The Levant, home of the earliest settlements, includes the Dead Sea, the Jordan Valley, and the surrounding foothills and coastal plain of present-day Israel, Lebanon, and Syria. To the west and north of the crescent lie the Taurus Mountains and the Anatolian Plateau of Turkey. The western portions of the crescent are defined by the Zagros mountain region, which is bounded on the east by the Diyala plain of west-central Iran. Cradled in the bosom of the crescent is the drainage of the Tigris and Euphrates rivers, which flow from the mountains of eastern Turkey, Syria, and northern Iraq into the desert floodplain of southern Iraq, before emptying into the Persian Gulf.

The northern portion of this drainage, which includes the foothills and fertile intermontane valleys of northern Iraq, was known as Upper Mesopotamia. The southern drainage, where the Tigris and Euphrates converge and eventually join into the Shatt-al-Arab waterway leading into the Persian Gulf, was known as Lower Mesopotamia. To the south lies the huge expanse of the Arabian Desert.

EARLY VILLAGES (LATE MESOLITHIC TO EARLY NEOLITHIC)

Toward the end of the Pleistocene, some 11,000 years ago, changing environmental conditions prompted wandering groups of Mesolithic (Middle Stone Age) hunter-gatherers to settle into small communities, where they took the first steps toward the domestication of certain species of plants and animals. At first, this involved the simple harvesting of large stands of wild wheat and the herding of sheep and goats. These early changes are evident at several settlements where archaeologists have recovered sickle blades and milling stones used in the harvesting and processing of plant foods, and large quantities of bones, primarily from wild sheep and goats that were held in captivity. Initially, these activities were only a supplement to the mainstream of daily life, which still focused on hunting and foraging. Most of these early hamlets are found in the Levant, where they formed part of the Natufian culture. Natufian settlements consisted of clusters of semisubterranean, circular pit-houses and storage pits, sometimes accompanied by cemeteries. Grave goods included seashells, stone bowls, and obsidian artifacts, indicating the beginnings of social ranking and intercommunity trade.

The earliest civilizations of the Near East were centered in the Fertile Crescent, a great semicircle of hills and valleys that stretches from the southern Levant to western Iran *(right)*. **However, it was in the region of southern Iraq known as Sumeria, that the first cities emerged. The small inset map** *(below)* **shows the major settlements of ancient Sumeria.**

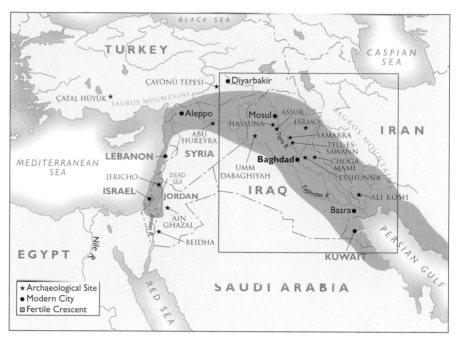

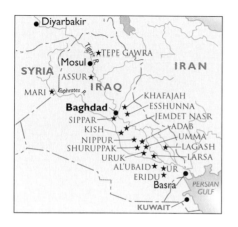

Eventually, between 9000 and 7000 B.C., permanent communities with a heavy dependence on cultivation and animal husbandry began appearing in the Fertile Crescent. This was the flowering of a new way of life, known as the Neolithic period, or New Stone Age. The remains of these early village-farming cultures have been identified at a number of locations, most notably at Jericho in the Jordan Valley, at Beidha and 'Ain Ghazal in Jordan, Ali Kosh in western Iran, Jarmo in Iraq, Abu Hureyra in Syria, and Çayönü Tepesi in eastern Turkey. At several of these sites, excavations have documented the transition from an initial experimentation with wild plants and animals to the full-time cultivation of several varieties of domestic wheat and the domestication of herds of sheep and goats. These early settlements often began as small hamlets of circular or oval pithouses, and eventually grew into substantial communities of rectangular, one-story, mud-brick houses, with several hundred inhabitants.

Although most of these communities appear to have been homogeneous clusters of domestic units of tribal farmers, at one site there is evidence of more complex activities. At the early site of Jericho, which covered some 10 acres (4 hectares), excavations have uncovered a 9-foot-deep (3-meter-deep) ditch and an adjoining wall with a tower, which may have surrounded the village. While it is not clear whether these constructions served defensive or flood control purposes, they do reflect a substantial investment of labor, which in turn suggests the emergence of rudimentary forms of social, political, and economic complexity.

The town of Jericho, located in a natural oasis in the Jordan Valley close to the Dead Sea, is the site of one of the world's earliest known permanent settlements. Excavation of the group of mounds shown in the photograph at right has unearthed evidence of a circular ditch, stone wall, and tower dated to around 8000 B.C. At far right, a section of the excavated area shows part of the city's walls. The massive stone tower, visible at the lower right of the photograph, was built within the walls, presumably as part of the city's defenses.

By 6000 B.C., early Neolithic settlements had spread throughout the Near East. Along with the growth of a village-farming way of life came the beginnings of craftsmanship and simple technology. The first pottery appeared around 7000 B.C., and spread quickly throughout the region. Craftsmen also began experimenting with the shaping of artifacts from copper. The quick diffusion of these technologies is a clear indication of the growing communication between these communities, a pattern also reflected in the appearance of trade goods from distant sources: seashells from the Mediterranean and Red Sea coasts are found at many sites in the interior, and obsidian from the mountains of Turkey reached deep into the southern Levant and to the Zagros Mountains in the east.

Obsidian, a volcanic glass used to produce sharp-edged tools, was a prominent commodity in early Near Eastern trade, and gave rise to one of the most complex early settlements in the region. Çatal Hüyük, a site in southern Turkey, derived its prosperity from a monopoly of the obsidian sources in the nearby mountains. This community—which can now be called a town—covered 32

acres (13 hectares), and was made up of a dense concentration of adjoining, sun-dried, mud-brick structures set around small courtyards. Excavations carried out by archaeologist James Mellaart in the 1960s uncovered several shrines with wall paintings and altars decorated with sculpted bull heads and benches with horns, and relief models of bulls and rams. Prominent themes in the artwork include figurines and paintings of bulls and women, and, in some cases, scenes of women giving birth to bulls. These early shrines, with their heavy focus on bulls and fertility, were most likely the forerunners of similar themes in the later art and religion of the Bronze Age Aegean cultures, particularly the cult of the Minotaur of the Minoan civilization.

LATE NEOLITHIC SETTLEMENTS IN MESOPOTAMIA

Following the growth of villages and towns in the Levant and Turkey, the path towards greater complexity shifts to Mesopotamia. The first large villages in Mesopotamia appeared in the north, spreading from the foothills of the Zagros Mountains to the northern edge of the Tigris-Euphrates floodplain,

Several shrines, similar to the one reconstructed here, have been uncovered in the settlement of Çatal Hüyük, in Turkey. Common to them all is a prominent decorative theme of rams, bulls' heads, and horns, which are thought to have fertility and religious associations. The illustration at far right depicts the plan of an excavated section of Çatal Hüyük dating from 6000 B.C. The closely packed mud-brick dwellings were set around small courtyards.

and formed part of a regional development known as the Hassunan culture (circa 6000 B.C. to 5000 B.C.). The site that gave its name to the culture is Hassuna, today a *tepe* (mound) some 165 yards by 220 yards (150 by 200 meters) across, located 8.5 miles (14 kilometers) south of Mosul in northern Iraq. This community, one of the first Neolithic sites excavated in Mesopotamia, was carefully laid out. The buildings consisted of rectangular rooms set around courtyards with ovens and grain bins. Similar site plans have been uncovered at several sites in the region, including Samarra, Tell-es-Sawwan, Choga Mami, and Umm Dabaghiyah.

Of all these sites, the best known is Umm Dabaghiyah, which was excavated by Diana Kirkbride in the late 1960s and early 1970s. The settlement is made up of dozens of rectilinear rooms arranged around courtyards. The

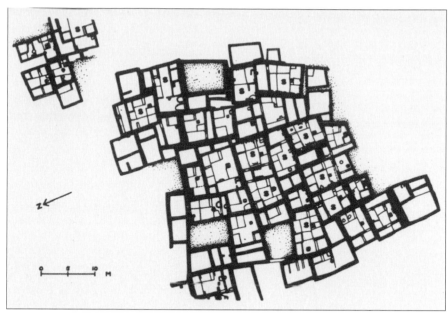

floors were made of gypsum plaster, and the walls of pressed mud; the walls often included niches, used, perhaps, for storing food. Many of the buildings were houses, with easily identified living rooms and kitchens, and, in some instances, ovens with chimneys. Several houses had the remains of frescoes, one of which displayed a hunting scene. Other groups of rooms, laid in double rows, lack residential features, and may have been used for storage. The economy of Umm Dabaghiyah appears to have been based on a mixture of agriculture, hunting, and trade. Among the staple crops were emmer wheat, einkorn wheat, and barley; domesticated animals included sheep, goats, cattle, and pigs. Hunting was an important part of daily life, judging from the large amounts of remains of onager, a type of wild ass, and gazelle. The hides of these animals may have been traded to other communities. In return, the villagers imported flint and obsidian for making tools, as well as artifacts made from basalt, greenstone, and seashells. Other artifacts include spindle whorls for spinning wool, clay figurines, and a variety of decorated pottery.

Hassunan ceramics, mostly bowls and jars, exhibit varied decorative techniques, including slipping, burnishing, painting, appliqué, and incision. As would be expected in the earliest decorated pottery, there is a great deal of experimentation, with painted and incised geometric designs, dots, wavy lines, and circles, as well as appliquéd human and animal faces and heads. Much of the fancier pottery at Hassunan sites is found in graves. These also contain many of the above-mentioned trade items, as well as baked-clay figurines, polished beads, and alabaster bowls and statuettes. The elaborate goods found in the graves of infants and small children suggest inherited social rank, a clear indication of the emergence of social stratification.

Most Hassunan communities are found in the foothills of the Zagros Mountains, where dry farming is possible. However, a later group of sites, known collectively as the Samarran culture, are found farther to the south, in drier regions. This southern expansion was made possible by the development of irrigation, which was to be a critical factor in the eventual settlement of Lower Mesopotamia. Excavations at the Samarran site of Choga Mami, near Mandali in eastern Iraq, have revealed traces of a primitive irrigation system, the oldest in the world. This was a large site, covering 2.5 acres (1 hectare), and is estimated to have had a population of more than 1000 people. While the intensification of agriculture through irrigation allowed for the expansion and construction of larger communities in the south, there is some evidence to suggest that the inhabitants had concerns beyond subsistence. At Choga Mami, a tower stands next to one of the town entrances, while at Tell-es-Sawwan—to the northwest, on the Tigris River—excavations have uncovered the remains of a ditch and wall around part of the town. These appear to be fortifications, suggesting that these early communities came under attack; from whom and for what reason we can only guess: other settlements competing for land or trade routes, perhaps, or nomadic raiders in search of food and craft goods.

It is probably no coincidence that irrigation and fortifications appeared at the same time in ancient Mesopotamia. Irrigation permitted many farmers to invest more energy into the production of craft goods, which in turn allowed for the growth of surplus wealth and the beginnings of social ranking. The accumulation of new wealth most likely created tensions between competing groups and communities, and may have attracted outside raiding groups as well. The town planning, irrigation, and defense systems, and the trade networks that developed in the Hasunnan period undoubtedly called for management and leadership skills, and most likely gave rise to a rudimentary ruling class, in which each community was ruled by a chief and his cohorts.

The expansion to the south gave rise to a new culture, known as the Halafian, around 5500 B.C. This culture, which overlapped with the Hassunan, is characterized by a more sophisticated, uniform ceramic style and a distinctive architectural tradition. Only a few Halafian sites have been excavated, but the similarity in the painted designs on their pottery is remarkable; sites as far apart as 340 miles (550 kilometers) often have identical forms and decorative motifs. Halafian architecture included larger structures with stone foundations, including circular buildings with an antechamber, resulting in a keyhole design. There is also a pronounced increase in the quantities of craft goods and trade items found at Halafian sites. Among the more prominent new artifacts are clay and stone stamp and cylinder seals with a variety of geometric designs (which had appeared earlier in small numbers at a few Samarran sites). Seals were probably used to stamp individualized motifs on personal property, and were widely used in trade.

Once the focal point of the community it served, the Eanna Ziggurat at Uruk, in present-day Iraq, still rises boldly above the landscape. Although badly eroded, this pyramid was once surrounded by courtyards and terraces, and its temple was dedicated to the goddess of heaven.

By 5300 B.C., a mixed Hassunan/Samarran/Halafian culture had reached into the southern Mesopotamian plain, assisted by the spread of irrigation. By 5000 B.C., we begin to see a common cultural horizon across greater Mesopotamia, from the Mediterranean to western Iran. The uniformity of ceramic and architectural styles suggests widespread interaction throughout the region, likely through trade between the elites of different communities. Several scholars have suggested that these changes reflect a fundamental transition in Near Eastern cultures from that of a tribal organization to a chiefdom-level society, with ranked kin groups and elites directing surplus labor and resources into larger public projects, such as irrigation systems. These developments set the stage for the rise of a more complex society, one that would lead to the world's first city-states.

ON THE THRESHOLD OF URBANISM: THE FIRST REAL TOWNS

The earliest known settlement in Lower Mesopotamia was at Eridu, where archaeologists have uncovered the remains of a small mud-brick village dating back to 5300 B.C. This marks the beginning of the Ubaid period (5300 B.C. to 3900 B.C.), a time of explosive growth in the south. The excavations at Eridu, begun by Iraqi archaeologists and by the English archaeologist Seton Lloyd in the 1940s, revealed some of the earliest monumental public architecture in the Near East: a series of superimposed temples that may have been dedicated to Enki, the god of water. The earliest of these was a simple shrine, which was later expanded into a large building set on a platform with an entry staircase, leading into a main room with two large altars; several smaller rooms flanked the central precinct. The town grew around the temples; by the end of the period, Eridu covered 25 acres (10 hectares), and had an estimated population of 2000 to 4000 people.

Throughout the region, as villages grew into towns, many new settlements appeared. Among the larger communities were Eridu, Al 'Ubaid, and Uruk (also known as Warka), in the south, and Tepe Gawra in the far north. An interesting pattern that emerges from regional survey patterns at this time is evidence of immigration from rural areas into the larger towns. Halafian ceramics and artifacts from the north appear increasingly in southern towns during this period, as do cultural elements such as pottery and other artifacts from the Susiana Plain in Iranian Khuzistan. It is also likely that nomadic tribal groups from the nearby highland areas of the Zagros may have also been attracted to the new towns. This pattern of rural-urban migration continues to this day, and is one of the principal causes of growth in modern cities throughout the world.

The growth of Mesopotamian towns continued during the following Uruk and Jemdet Nasr periods (3900 B.C. to 2900 B.C.). These communities exhibit a growing distinction between large public buildings and common residences, and further evidence of increasing craft specialization and social differentiation. By this time, towns had become crowded settlements, with large buildings, painted temples, courtyards, and alleyways. Large temples on platforms, known as ziggurats, became the dominant structures of the larger communities. The ziggurats appear to have been the seat of power of rulers who directed a complex hierarchy of aristocrats, priests, bureaucrats, and merchants, who in turn managed the economy and daily life of thousands of craftsmen, construction workers, farmers, herdsmen, sailors, and fishermen who made up the bulk of the population of the towns and their surrounding areas.

One of the best-known sites of the period, and likely one of the largest, was Uruk, which was first settled in the previous Ubaid period. Excavations undertaken since 1899 by a series of German expeditions have uncovered a substantial metropolis of approximately 200 acres (80 hectares) in area, with an estimated population of 10,000 people. The site contained two central clusters of monumental architecture known as the Anu Ziggurat and the Eanna Precinct. The ziggurat is an imposing structure, a high platform accessed by a series of ramps and stairways. On top lay the White Temple, a well-preserved brick building containing a central hall flanked by two rows of rooms. At one end of the hall was a large pedestal that may have served as an altar; at the other was a platform, with ascending steps, which may have been a base for a large statue. The temple is believed to have been dedicated to the worship of the sky-god Anu, the supreme deity of the Sumerian pantheon. The Eanna Precinct contains several structures, including a colonnaded hallway, a court paved with mosaics, and a large rectangular building known as the Limestone Temple. This last was a massive construction, built on a base of limestone blocks, which measured more than 90 feet (30 meters) in width by 220 feet (67 meters) in length. The Eanna Precinct was dedicated to the rituals of Inanna, the goddess of love and war, who was the patron deity of Uruk.

The massive public projects of Uruk and other settlements were the outcome of an increasingly centralized administration of an economy that was fueled by a growing population, increased food production, and major innovations in crafts and technology. Archaeological surveys of the surrounding countryside indicate that a hierarchy of settlements began to form around the larger communities, supplying them with labor and agricultural products. Extensive irrigation networks, fed by large canals, were laid out, often replacing smaller, local systems. These large networks may have been planned and built by an emerging state apparatus. The invention of the ox-driven plow further increased agricultural production. Other major inventions included the potter's wheel, which quickly led to mass-produced pottery, wheeled vehicles for land transport and trade, and the sailboat, for fishing and trade on the rivers and in the Persian Gulf. The growing economy produced another invention: by 3400 B.C., the first clay tablets with a rudimentary pictographic script appeared. By the end of the period, many of the pictographs had acquired phonetic values, a transformation that would lead to the world's earliest form of writing, a hieroglyphic script known as cuneiform. The earliest clay tablets did not recount historic events; rather, they were used for recording business transactions and for accounting records.

By 2900 B.C., a centrally controlled temple economy was in place, and several of the towns had grown into full-fledged cities. The overall political picture still eludes us, but there is strong evidence to suggest that the cities were ruled by kings who controlled substantial surrounding territories, indicating that a state level of organization had emerged. Full development of the state came in the following Early Dynastic period.

THE CITIES OF SUMER

Mesopotamia enters recorded history at the onset of the Early Dynastic period (2900 B.C. to 2400 B.C.). A series of documents known as the Sumerian King Lists, engraved on clay tablets in the late third millennium, provide an account of ancient kings going back thousands of years. While many of the early kings are mythical figures, scholars have identified dynastic lineages that emerged at several cities after 2900 B.C. The best-documented early dynasties are those of Kish, Uruk, Ur, and Lagash. Most of the information pertains to the region that came to be known as Sumer, which includes all of Mesopotamia south of

The partially reconstructed Ziggurat of Ur, in the lower left corner of this aerial view, rises above the excavated outlines of the great Sumerian city's buildings. Ur was a relatively compact city, and its densely packed buildings were connected by a web of winding alleys, with some avenues laid out on a grid plan. Located around the ziggurat, at the city's center, were the major public buildings, temples, and residences of the elite.

Baghdad; during this period, the political landscape crystalized into a mosaic of densely settled city-states.

At least 16 cities developed in Sumer proper. These included Eridu, Ur, Lagash, Nippur, Uruk, Larsa, Umma, Al 'Ubaid, Jemdet Nasr, Bad-Tibira, Shuruppak, Adab, Larak, Kish, Assur, and Sippar. In northern Mesopotamia, several communities also reached urban proportions and shared a common culture with that of Sumer; the most important of these were Khafajah, Esshnunna, Mari, and Tepe Gawra. The size of the Sumerian cities varied considerably. Ur, a relatively small city, covered some 150 acres (60 hectares); Nippur extended over 800 acres (320 hectares), while Uruk may have spread 1100 acres (450 hectares)—a little under 2 square miles (5.18 square kilometers). The population of most cities is estimated at 10,000 to 20,000, with a few larger ones, such as Uruk, with perhaps as many as 50,000 people.

At the onset of Early Dynastic times, Sumer also had a large number of sizeable rural communities as well. Archaeologist Robert McC. Adams, who has conducted extensive surveys of the region, estimates that more than 80 percent

28

The British archaeologist Sir Leonard Woolley undertook the reconstruction of the Ziggurat of Ur in the 1930s. At right, his meticulous work on the first level can be seen, with the contours of the central stairway set off against the massive, buttressed walls. The illustration below, based on Woolley's partial reconstruction, shows the three stairways converging at a covered gateway that gave access to the upper levels. The elevated temple at the top is thought to have been the focus of the structure.

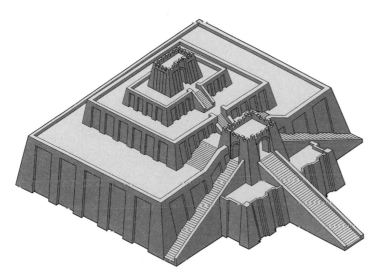

of the Sumerian population lived in rural communities of 25 or more acres (10 hectares). The rural population eventually declined—to 50 percent by 2000 B.C.—as many of the inhabitants moved into the larger cities. The size of the territory of individual city-states is not known, but it is likely that each controlled several hundred square miles. Estimates for the population of all of Sumer, including urban and rural areas, are in the range of several hundred thousand, perhaps half a million, which yields a density of 52 people per square mile (20 per square kilometer).

The Sumerian city was an impressive sight to behold. Many of the cities were surrounded by walls, as was the case at Ur and Uruk. The great wall of Uruk was almost 6 miles (9.5 kilometers) in length, and had a double rampart; the inner wall was more than 12 feet (4 meters) thick. The city gates were flanked by large rectangular towers, and a series of semicircular bastions dotted the wall at intervals along its entire length. Inside the walls was a densely packed mass of brick buildings, mostly rectangular in layout, with occasional courtyards and a web of winding alleys. In some cases, streets were laid out in grid fashion. Towards the center of the city were the public buildings, often enclosed by walls. The focal point of the city was the ziggurat.

The Great Ziggurat of Ur, built by King Ur-nammu of the Third Dynasty of Ur (2113 B.C. to 2096 B.C.), is one of the best preserved of these structures. The ziggurat, which has been partially restored, consisted of an

enormous three-tiered platform, with a base measuring 140 feet by 200 feet (43 by 62 meters), and was over 85 feet (26 meters) in height; the top can be reached by a series of staircases, the most imposing of which is a central staircase flanked by a massive stepped balustrade. The temple on top has not survived, but we know from other structures what it must have looked like. The ziggurat temple was the home of the patron deity of the city, and generally consisted of a large hallway flanked by rows of rooms on each side. The hall contained a large platform holding a statue of the god or goddess, and an altar for performing sacrifices. The exterior of the temple was decorated with multicolored cone mosaics—conical bricks set into the walls— relief panels, and statues of animals. Some of the panels were made of wood and covered with copper sheeting.

Surrounding the ziggurat were clusters of other public buildings, including royal palaces, temples, administrative buildings, archives, and storerooms. From this downtown core, main streets radiated out to the city gates. The houses of the elite were located along these streets, and the rest of the town was taken up by residences of the commoners. Originally, most houses were simple, single-story homes with two or three rooms. In later times, those who could afford it built two-storied structures with additional rooms, often set around a courtyard. Another feature of Sumerian cities was their cemeteries, and the most famous of these is the Royal Cemetery of Ur, excavated by Sir Leonard Woolley between 1927 and 1931. This cemetery consisted of a network of vaulted subterranean chambers in which royal corpses were placed in wagons or chariots with a rich array of goods. They were accompanied by the oxen that drew them and the bodies of several retainers; one royal grave was accompanied by the remains of

Almost every Sumerian temple that has been excavated has yielded large numbers of votive statues like the scribe shown above. The hands of these figures are invariably folded as if in prayer. From the dedicatory inscriptions found carved on each one, it is thought that the statues represent effigies of individual worshippers that were placed in the temples to intercede with the gods.

63 people, including drivers, soldiers, musicians, courtiers, and courtesans. The graves contained some of the richest artifacts found in the ancient world: solid gold bowls and goblets, a solid gold helmet, musical instruments made of wood inlaid with shell and lapis lazuli, and exotic statuary and jewelry made from gold, silver, copper, and lapis lazuli.

Clay tablets tell us a great deal about the society of ancient Sumerian cities. At the top of the social pyramid were the king and the nobility, priests (and occasionally priestesses) and their scribes, the top members of the military, and the wealthier merchants. Originally, the vast majority of the commoner class was primarily concerned with the production of food and with construction, and included farmers, herdsmen, and fishermen. As the city grew more complex, many of the commoners began to take on full-time specializations; among these were merchants, potters, stonemasons, carpenters, metalworkers, basketweavers, leatherworkers, wool spinners and tailors, and bakers and brewers. There was also a class of slaves, consisting mostly of laborers who worked in farming or construction or as servants to the elite and assistants to the specialists. The growing numbers of craft specialists made the population more diverse, and formed the basis for increasingly complex social rankings and social stratification.

The craft specialists produced an impressive array of goods, from everyday items such as pottery and clothing to fancy stone jewelry and metal objects. Sumerian smiths worked copper, gold, silver, and lead, and were the first to manufacture bronze, made from an alloy of tin and copper—giving rise to the term Bronze Age. Metals were used to produce a variety of tools and weapons, helmets, cups and bowls, statues, ornaments, and jewelry.

Transport and trade were important pillars of the Sumerian economy. Wheeled vehicles and sailing vessels were increasingly used to transport goods, and trading expeditions spread throughout the Near East, overland from the Mediterranean to eastern Iran, and to the farther reaches of the Persian Gulf and beyond. At Ur, canals and a harbor were built to handle traffic on the Euphrates River; the city was also a major port of entry for shipping from the Persian Gulf. As Lower Mesopotamia was deficient in mineral resources and timber, most of its trade involved the exchange of manufactured goods for raw materials. Tablets record that the main exports from Sumer were textiles, though they also included many craft goods. Imports included timber from the Zagros Mountains and from Lebanon; copper, silver, arsenic, and tin from Turkey, Iran, and the Persian Gulf; gold from Syria, Anatolia, and Iran; and carnelian and soapstone from Iran. The Sumerians maintained an extensive maritime trade network in the Persian Gulf; historic texts mention heavy trading activities with Elam (southwest Iran), Dilmun (modern Bahrain), Magan (Oman), and Meluhha (the Indus region). Magan was a major source of copper, while Meluhha supplied tin and lapis lazuli from Afghanistan.

Many of the key features that characterize the development of the ancient Western world can be traced to the accomplishments of the ancient Sumerians. While their technical inventions revolutionized the daily life of the human species, they also left behind a rich legacy of accomplishments in the arts and sciences, education, law, and religion. The development of writing was a fundamental contribution to the development of knowledge. While the early records were devoted primarily to bookkeeping, later texts contain a dazzling array of information. These texts include historical documents, myths, legal codes and documents, medical records, mathematical and astronomical texts, literary works, and treatises dealing with matters of religion. While the bulk of these materials were recorded after the Sumerian period proper—after 2400 B.C.—they offer a broad perspective on the cultural life of the Sumerians and their descendants. Education was available only to the male children of the elite, who attended schools and learned much of their subject matter from clay tablets containing grammars, mathematical tables, and lists of words describing different kinds of plants and animals, stones and minerals, and place-names. The primary purpose of this education was to learn to read and write the Sumerian language, which was essential for employment in the bureaucracy and priesthood. The world's first legal codes were drafted in Mesopotamia around 2100 B.C. These and later versions prescribe punishments for crimes, and include laws relating to marriage, divorce, inheritance, the sale and ownership of property and slaves, and a variety of other civil matters. Legal wrangles were resolved in courts with one or more judges, who were respected members of the community.

Sumerian religion evolved out of a polytheistic pantheon whose principal deities were the gods of air (Enlil), water (Enki), earth (Ki), and heaven (An). There were also gods of the sun, moon, and planets, of rivers, lakes, winds and storms, of many everyday things (such as tools and bricks), and even personal gods. There were rituals in the temples and celebrations dedicated to many of the gods, and major annual ceremonies to honor the chief deities. Each city had a patron deity who owned the community and ruled the lives of its inhabitants. For the people, the main purpose was to serve the gods and follow their divine orders. After death, souls passed to a fantastic netherworld beneath the earth ruled by deities who sat in judgment of all mortals. This, in a nutshell, is the reason for the strong religious focus of early Sumerian society: most aspects of daily life, even the economy of the city-state, revolved around the temple.

The evolution of political institutions is closely related to the temple. In the early days of Sumer, the cities were ruled by governors and an assembly of leading citizens, mostly merchants and landowners whose business was closely tied to the temple. As city-states began to compete for land, warfare became increasingly widespread, and a military class emerged. From this class arose the first strong rulers, who eventually became hereditary kings. In due course, the kings built large armies, surrounded themselves with a court and great wealth, and became increasingly independent from the temple. Still, a tension

One of many sumptuous artifacts unearthed by Sir Leonard Woolley during his excavations of the Royal Cemetry at Ur between 1927 and 1931 was this rampant he-goat, made of wood and delicately sheathed in gold, silver, and lapis lazuli. One of a pair found at the site, it is thought to symbolize plant and animal fertility.

always existed between the temple and the state, as one could not rule without the other. The king was the supreme civil and religious leader, and had to strike a balance between the religious concerns of the temple and the affairs of the state.

Warfare played a prominent role in the rise of Sumerian city-states. Historical documents indicate that the first cities were frequently at war with one another, often over highly prized land that was suitable for irrigation. Wars between cities continued sporadically throughout the Early Dynastic period, culminating in a series of conquests by Lugalzagesi, the king of Umma, who subjugated all of Sumer around 2400 B.C. His rule was short-lived, as he was defeated a few years later by King Sargon of Akkad (a city whose location has yet to be identified). With his successors, Sargon created a much larger nation-state that included all of Mesopotamia and adjoining Elam in western Iran. The Sargonid or Akkadian Period lasted until about 2200 B.C., when it was overthrown by a northern nomadic people known as the Guti. Following almost a century of anarchy, Sumer was again reunited in 2113 B.C. by Ur-nammu, King and founder of the Third Dynasty of Ur, which held sway until 2096 B.C. After this dynasty collapsed, Mesopotamia again became a mosaic of small city-states, until the emergence of the Babylonian state, which under Hammurabi came to control most of the Near East around 1700 B.C., thus establishing the world's first empire.

THE RISE OF THE SUMERIAN CITY-STATES

It is no surprise that all of V. Gordon Childe's defining characteristics of urbanism are found in ancient Sumer. After all, he based his list largely on historic and archaeological data from the Near East. Subsequent research has confirmed that many of the factors that he and other early scholars posited for the rise of the early state did, in fact, play a prominent role in Mesopotamia. These include the role of irrigation (without which Sumer would not have been settled), which led to the production of agricultural surpluses, which in turn allowed for increased craft production and trade, increased concentrations of wealth, social stratification, the emergence of kingship, and a state apparatus. It is also clear that population growth was a vital part of the whole process, acting both as cause and effect. Another prominent factor, likely brought on by demographic pressure and competition over resources, was warfare; as conflicts increased in frequency, warfare developed a life of its own, leading to the entrenchment of a military elite that enhanced the power of the king and state.

Most scholars would now agree that the above variables form the basic building blocks in the formation of the earliest Near Eastern states. A multi-factorial "systems-ecological" model tracing the complex interrelationship between these variables has been constructed by archaeologist Charles Redman and is illustrated on the opposite page.

Still, one may ask if any one factor, or group of factors, played a larger role in the evolution of the state than any others. While some factors are clearly more important than others—irrigation is more important than trade, for example—the relationship between other variables is not so clear. For example, did population growth lead to agricultural intensification, or was it the other way around? Until we have more detailed data from the field, such questions will remain in the domain of the proverbial chicken and egg. Still, it is questions like these that drive research. One way of exploring such puzzles is to look at other civilizations.

34

THE RISE OF CIVILIZATION

In 1978, archaeologist Charles Redman of Arizona State University developed what he termed a "systems-ecological" model to explain the rise of civilization in Mesopotamia. This model incorporated many of the causal factors that had been advanced by earlier theorists. Redman arranged these factors in a non-linear, multifactorial systems framework (shown below), and described the development of civiliza-tion as the outcome of "a series of incre-mental processes that were triggered by favorable ecological and cultural condi-tions and that continued to develop through mutually reinforcing interac-tions. The developmental process com-prised five positive-feedback interrelationships, three of which (A, B, and C) were prompted by the ecology and gave rise to the institutions that characterized early Mesopotamian cities. The fourth and fifth positive-feedback relationships (D and E) were themselves stimulated by early urban developments and helped to transform independent cities into members of a centralized national state." Another less tangible but fundamentally important variable was religion, which provided the glue that held the social institutions of ancient Mesopotamia—as well as those of other ancient societies—together.

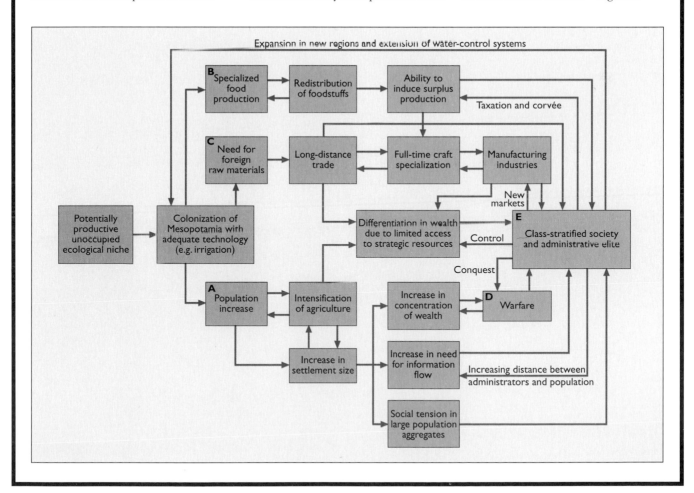

Beginning in the First Dynasty, the ancient Egyptians buried their nobility in the necropolis at Giza. During the Fourth Dynasty, however, three pyramids as their memorials, thus overshadowing the burial-ground custom and changing the desert landscape forever.

3

EGYPT: PYRAMID CITIES OF THE NILE

Around 3100 B.C., about the same time that Uruk was growing into a full-fledged city-state in Lower Mesopotamia, an urban society also was emerging in Egypt. Visions of early civilization in Egypt conjure up images of enormous pyramids and grandiose monuments, but cities are rarely part of the picture. Travelers to Egypt visit the pyramids and palaces of the pharaohs, and beyond these see little else but sand dunes. Popular books on ancient Egypt present the same vision, and the inevitable

pharaohs ordered the construction of mighty

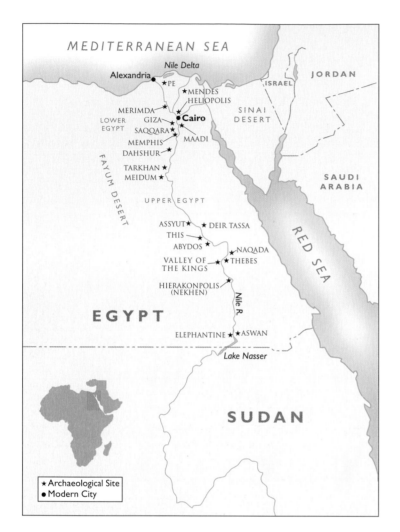

Sandwiched between cruel deserts, the civilization of ancient Egypt took root along the slender ribbon of the Nile Valley, between Aswan and the Mediterranean Sea. The map above shows the most important early Egyptian settlements.

question arises again and again: did anyone actually live around the pyramids? In some of the older reconstructions of Egyptian society, the pharaohs and their retainers lived in grandiose isolation in palaces around the pyramids, while villages scattered along the banks of the Nile River provided them with food and labor. This view of ancient Egypt as a non-urban society was so pervasive that at least two major popular books on the world's earliest cities, written in the 1970s, do not even include a section on Egypt.

Early hieroglyphic texts and a growing body of archaeological evidence indicate that urban settlements—sometimes called "temple towns"—were indeed part of the Egyptian landscape. We know very little about these early settlements (compared to, say, contemporary Mesopotamian cities), as most of them were destroyed in later periods or buried under the silt of the Nile and the shifting sands of the surrounding deserts. Still, the emergence of urbanism, although perhaps a slower and somewhat later development than in Mesopotamia, was a major feature of early Egyptian civilization.

Until recently, most archaeological work in Egypt has focused on the pyramids, palaces, and monuments of the various Dynastic periods after 3000 B.C.; little was known of the Predynastic periods. As a result, the crystalization of the Egyptian state was seen as an abrupt phenomenon, where civilization appeared suddenly in a region that hitherto had known only small farming villages. Beginning in the 19th century, this view gave rise to the notion that Egyptian civilization must have been the result of external influences or even of outright invasions from Mesopotamia. This diffusionist view has had many adherents, most recently among them Walter Emery, whose 1961 book, *Archaic Egypt*, argued that a master race from Mesopotamia laid the foundations of Egyptian civilization. This view is no longer widely held, as there is little evidence to support it. Predynastic Egypt probably imported some plant and animal domesticates and the notion of metalworking from southwest Asia, but evidence of heavy contact at the time of state formation is limited; there is evidence of trade and sustained contacts between Egypt and the Levant, and, to a lesser extent, to Mesopotamia, in Late Predynastic and Early Dynastic times, but not enough to justify massive cultural diffusion. In fact,

The fertile "black lands" of the Nile Valley—formed from silt deposited during the annual floods—made possible the development of civilization in ancient Egypt. The river's floodplain varies in width, with its greatest extent in Lower Egypt north of Aswan and in the Delta area. As this photograph shows, beyond the narrow, life-giving floodplain loom pitiless expanses of desert.

Egyptian culture—art and architecture, religion, social and political organization—is so different from that of the Sumerians that there is little ground for close comparison. Recent archaeological evidence also has undermined the diffusionist view by uncovering a long sequence of Predynastic developments that belies the notion of a "sudden" appearance of civilization. This sequence has its beginnings in early Neolithic settlements dating to 5000 B.C., and follows a gradual trajectory of growth and development leading up to the early pharaonic dynasties. As a result of this research, most scholars now see Egyptian civilization as a unique and highly indigenous creation and a monumental achievement in the annals of world history.

Egyptian civilization was forged in a single ecological crucible—the Nile River. The Greek historian Herodotus called Egypt "the gift of the Nile," for without its life-giving waters human settlement would not be possible. In fact, the vast majority of Egypt's population, from Paleolithic hunter-gatherers to modern city dwellers, has lived in the Valley of the Nile, known since ancient times as the "black lands" because of the rich, dark soils of the river's alluvium. In places, the floodplain can be as wide as 15 miles (24 kilometers). Beyond it lies only desert, the "red land," which, save for the occasional oasis, is mostly unfit for human habitation.

The Nile proper begins at the confluence of the Blue Nile and White Nile rivers in Sudan, and flows north through Nubia into Egypt until it reaches the waters of Lake Nasser, which was formed by the great dam built in the

1960s at Aswan. The core of Egyptian civilization developed along the river valley between Aswan and the Mediterranean Sea, a distance of 750 miles (1200 kilometers). The southern reaches of the Nile brought ancient Egyptians into contact with the kingdoms of Nubia, which were a rich source of trade goods from sub-Saharan Africa. From early times, the land of Egypt has been divided into two major regions: Upper Egypt, which stretches from Sudan to the Fayum Desert of northern Egypt; and Lower Egypt, where the river flows past Cairo and empties into the delta, dumping deep alluvial deposits that continue to provide farmers with rich agricultural lands. The floodplain is fairly narrow in Upper Egypt, and broadens considerably as it moves northward. The civilization of ancient Egypt also was shaped by its proximity to the Mediterranean and Red seas, both of which served as important conduits for trade to distant regions.

The history of Egyptology is quite extensive, and only a thumbnail sketch is possible here. Some of the oldest accounts of ancient Egypt have come down to us from Greek historians; Herodotus was one of the earliest such sources.

Intrigued by antiquities brought back by European travelers, Napoleon included scholars and artists in his expedition to Egypt in 1798. A colored engraving from a painting by Georges Clairin depicts a group of French officers admiring the statuary outside the temple at Karnak.

The lure of Egypt's magnificent tombs and monuments has drawn adventurers and scholars alike. In the early 19th century, the curiosity of the flamboyant Italian-born engineer Giovanni Battista Belzoni (*right*) led him to crawl through the rubble-choked passageways of dozens of tombs. His major feat was the procurement of the gigantic sculptured head of the Pharaoh Ramses II, which he shipped off to England. In contrast, British archaeologist William Flinders Petrie (*far right*) spent half a century excavating different sites in the Nile Valley. He amassed detailed records of all his findings, compiling data that has assisted Egyptologists the world over.

Later Roman and Arab travelers provided firsthand accounts of the ruins, and, beginning in the 15th century, we have accounts from European visitors. In the 18th century, Egyptology became a serious concern in Europe; travelers began to record the hieroglyphic inscriptions and bring back antiquities for growing museum collections. This demand for antiquities continued unabated into the late 19th century, and many sites were relentlessly plundered until an official Egyptian Antiquities Service was set up in 1881, requiring permits for all excavations. In 1798, Napoleon Bonaparte led a military expedition to Egypt, accompanied by a large contingent of scholars and artists who produced a series of volumes describing the ancient monuments. Among their discoveries was the famous Rosetta Stone, a monument that displayed parallel texts in Greek, hieroglyphic, and demotic scripts (the latter a late form of Egyptian writing). Several scholars immediately began working on its decipherment, and in 1822 a final breakthrough by the Frenchman Jean-François Champollion provided the key to the ancient hieroglyphic script.

The 19th century brought many expeditions to Egypt, including American, British, German, Italian, and Swiss, and produced a mass of scholarly literature. Their excavations focused mainly on the pyramids and royal tombs. Many of the explorers and archaeologists who participated in these expeditions were Indiana Jones-type characters, and their exploits provided the basis for endless romantic tales that were celebrated in novels, movies, and *New Yorker* cartoons. One of the more colorful explorers was Giovanni Belzoni, an Italian engineer who first entered the pyramid of King Khafre (Chephren) at Giza in 1818. Among the more serious scholars, none looms as large as Sir William Flinders Petrie, who dedicated half a century, from 1884 onwards, to surveying and excavating scores of sites throughout the Nile Valley. In the 20th century, work led by a host of Egyptian and foreign scholars has continued at many sites.

Although not trained in archaeology, Englishman Howard Carter spent years in the company of explorers in Egypt's Valley of the Kings. Carter's singleminded quest for the tomb of the boy-king Tutankhamun was finally rewarded in 1922, when he opened the ruler's burial chamber. Inside lay a hoard of priceless treasures.

One of the greatest discoveries in the history of Egyptology was made in 1922, when the Englishman Howard Carter uncovered the tomb of the Pharaoh Tutankhamun in the Valley of the Kings, near Thebes. Some of the largest excavation projects of recent times have been carried out by Egyptian scholars, most notably Selim Bey Hassan, Abdessalam Hussein, Zakaria Goneim, Ahmed Fakhry, and Kemal el Malakh, the last of whom, in the 1950s, uncovered the spectacular "solar boats," or funeral barques, at the Great Pyramid of Giza.

Before 1960, most Egyptian research was exploratory and descriptive in nature, and was aimed at reconstructing historic events and life in ancient times. In the last 35 years, several scholars have begun to develop a theoretical framework that examines the larger question of how and why early Egyptian society developed as it did. Their research has laid the foundation for exploring the processes that led to the emergence and growth of Egyptian civilization and urbanism, issues which we shall pursue in the pages that follow.

THE PREDYNASTIC PERIOD

The earliest inhabitants of the Nile Valley were nomadic foragers, who subsisted on a mixed economy of fishing, hunting, and gathering plants for several thousand years prior to the appearance of the first settled villages around 5000 B.C. The oldest Neolithic settlements, which have been discovered at Fayum and at Merimda near the delta, were simple clusters of semisubterranean pithouses, roofed with mud and sticks. Excavations have also uncovered hearths and grain-storage pits made from buried baskets or clay jars, as well as simple graves. The people cultivated barley and emmer wheat, and kept dogs, cattle, pigs, sheep, and goats. The idea of domesticating plants and animals was probably imported from southwest Asia, where domestication occurred much earlier. In fact, some domesticates, such as barley, wheat, sheep, and goats, were likely imported across the Sinai Peninsula from the Levant. Others, such as dogs, cattle, and pigs, may have been domesticated from local wild species.

The early Neolithic inhabitants made a simple undecorated pottery—mostly water jars and dishes—and wove baskets from rushes and wheat straw. Containers also were made from ostrich eggs. These early people used stone tools, mostly fashioned from flint, that included axes, knives, and arrowheads, the latter indicating the use of bows and arrows. Harpoons carved from bone were used in fishing. Both fishing and hunting added large amounts of meat to the diet, including that of elephants, hippopotamuses, and crocodiles, as well as that of a wide variety of smaller mammals, waterfowl, and reptiles. Boats and canoes, in use before 4500 B.C., greatly improved fishing and communication along the Nile.

We do not have very accurate estimates of the number of people living in these early Neolithic villages, but preliminary indications are that, by about 4000 B.C., the settlements had grown quite large. At that time, Merimda cov-

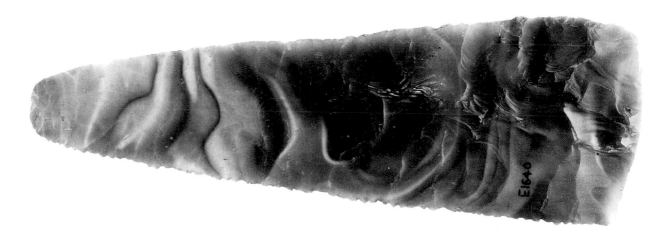

Flint tools, such as the knife shown above, were the principal implements of Egypt's earliest Neolithic communities. Flint was used for axes, knives, and arrowheads.

ered an area of 44 acres (18 hectares), and is estimated to have numbered between 900 and 2000 inhabitants.

Beginning around 4300 B.C., a group of some 80 Neolithic settlements and cemeteries, collectively known as the Badarian culture, appeared in Upper/Middle Egypt in the region south of Assyut. These had most of the same features as the northern villages, except that they were much smaller. One excavated village, Deir Tasa, covered only a little more than an acre (.5 hectare), and is estimated to have been populated by between 40 and 65 people. Badarian pottery is much more sophisticated than the earlier Neolithic pottery of the Fayum: decorative techniques used on the fancier wares included combing, burnishing, and polishing. Artifacts found at Badarian sites include awls and pins made from hammered copper, steatite beads from Palestine, shells from the Red Sea, turquoise from Libya or the Sinai Peninsula, and pine and cedar objects from Lebanon or Syria. Graves were simple oval or rectangular pits, covered with sticks or matting, and held one or more bodies protected by hides or fiber mats. Offerings included food, stone or ivory vases, ivory combs, and ivory and clay figurines.

In the period that followed (circa 4000 B.C. to 3000 B.C.), settlements along the Nile multiplied and grew, and a continuous string of villages gradually dotted the river between Aswan and the delta. Some of the older communities, such as Merimda, were abandoned, for reasons unknown. The subsistence economy was now based on full-time farming, with a pronounced decline in hunting; peas and vetch were added to the inventory of cultivated crops. After 3600 B.C., cultivation was improved by the use of rudimentary canals and dams, which enabled farmers to better defend themselves against the changing flood levels of the Nile. These floods, occurring almost annually, could easily wipe out large areas under cultivation. These forms of water management required no administrative apparatus beyond purely local management. In fact, irrigation technology was a simple matter well into the first millennium, and did not play a significant role in the rise of the state in Predynastic times, as it did in Mesopotamia.

A bas-relief from the Sixth Dynasty illustrates the timeless rhythm of life along the banks of the Nile. A group of farmers in a canoe lead their cattle through the water, while a variety of fish—and a crocodile—swim below the surface. Boats were used on the Nile from at least 4500 B.C., providing a more varied diet as well as better communications to early communities. Some animals, such as cattle and pigs, were probably domesticated from local wild species; others, including goats and sheep, were imported from the Levant sometime after 5000 B.C.

Some communities grew substantially, especially in the south. By 3500 B.C., a few had evolved into full-fledged towns. Two settlements in the Naqada region are estimated to have had between 800 and 900 inhabitants, while the burgeoning town of Hierakonpolis may have had as many as 1500 to 2000 people. Houses became more solid, and mud-brick structures eventually replaced the simple huts of earlier times. By 3500 B.C., rectangular mud-brick houses were quite common, and, towards the end of the period, the elite of some towns were building elaborate multiroomed homes.

The last few centuries of the Predynastic period saw significant advances in craft production and technology. Whole new styles of pottery appeared, with a wide array of vessel shapes and decorative techniques. The fancier wares, which often accompanied burials, were painted with a variety of patterns, and occasionally depicted scenes with people, animals, trees, and boats; many also had handles, lugs, and spouts. A few towns began to specialize in the mass production of pottery, which was manufactured on a hand-turned wheel.

Other crafts also prospered. The inventory of goods recovered from excavations includes finely worked flint tools, stone vessels ground out of basalt and alabaster, slate palettes (often carved in the shapes of animals), and beads and amulets carved out of exotic stone, including lapis lazuli. Metallurgy flourished during this period, as smiths experimented with copper, gold, and silver. The sources of these metals lay in the Eastern Desert of Upper Egypt (between the Nile and the Red Sea) and in the Sinai Peninsula; in later times, additional quantities of silver were imported from the Near East, and gold was brought down the Nile from Nubia. Coppersmiths produced a huge variety of hammered and cast ornaments, tools, and weapons, including spearheads, axes, daggers and knives, harpoons and fish hooks, and an assortment of jewelry. Gold and silver, used primarily in the manufacture of luxury goods and ornaments, were less common and highly prized. Bronze working did not figure in Egypt until much later; it appears to have been introduced from southwest Asia during the Middle Kingdom (1991 B.C. to 1785 B.C.).

Large sailing craft now plied the Nile, and many raw materials and manufactured craft goods were traded up and down the river. It appears that by Late Predynastic times, localized barter had given way to a formalized system of trade managed by professional merchants who employed scores of bearers and sailors. Caravans of donkeys also traveled the deserts, bearing goods from the Red Sea, the Sinai, and beyond. (Camels were not introduced into Egypt until Roman times.) At two locations in Lower Egypt, El-Omari and Maadi, excavations have yielded substantial evidence of long-distance trade. El-Omari is a complex of sites near Helwan, in the Nile Delta. Goods recovered here include necklaces and pendants made from Red Sea shells, and large quantities of stone tools that closely resemble those of the Levant. It has been suggested that El-Omari may have been a community of merchants involved in long-distance trade. The same may be true of the ancient delta port of Pe (later known by its Greek name, Buto), where ceramics and other artifacts also indicate contacts with southwest Asia. The evidence of such activity is more striking at Maadi, a town on a terrace of the Nile just south of Cairo. Here a large complex of subterranean storage cellars was found to contain a variety of food remains, local artifacts, and imports. These discoveries have led archaeologists to suggest that Maadi represented a commercial trade depot operated by long-distance merchants, perhaps including traders from southwest Asia. The underground chambers and huge storage jars have no precedent in Egypt, but closely resemble vessels found in Palestine. Among the imported goods are pottery from the Levant, and a type of chalice or cup likely made in contemporary Sumer. Egyptian ceramics and other trade goods are also found at corresponding sites in the Levant. In later times, colonies of Egyptian merchants appeared at several communities in Palestine and Lebanon; most prominent among these was the Lebanese port of Byblos, which maintained a regular maritime trade with Egypt; exports from the Levant included metals, timber (mostly cedar, for which Lebanon was famous), wine, and olive oil.

Upper Egypt also exhibits evidence of contacts with southwest Asia in Late Predynastic times. Several artistic motifs used in the decoration of stone palettes and ivory artifacts were adopted from Mesopotamia, and trade goods include a number of vessels and cylinder seals imported from Sumer. These motifs and trade goods were introduced into Upper Egypt by traders and artisans who came from southwest Asia via the delta and Lower Egypt; they were likely lured by the gold of the Eastern Desert, which was controlled and mined by the towns of Upper Egypt.

As the economy grew more complex, so also did Egyptian society. As was the case in Mesopotamia, the emergence of full-time specialists and merchants was a major source of social differentiation. Several archaeologists have also noted that craft production was spurred by a growing demand for luxury goods, reflecting the growth of a well-to-do class. Many of the craft goods were produced specifically as grave offerings for the elite, and by Late Predynastic times a formal funerary cult had arisen across Egypt.

Elite burials provide clear evidence of increasing social differentiation. Not only were the tombs larger and more elaborate, sometimes consisting of mud-brick chambers with painted walls, but the wealth of luxury goods was in some cases quite impressive. The burial of one man (most likely a local chief) at El-Omari included necklaces and pendants made from Red Sea shells, exotic stones, mother-of-pearl, and ostrich eggshell, as well as a wooden scepter similar to the staffs carried by later Egyptian kings. The painted scenes found in some of the more elaborate tombs in Upper Egypt—especially at Hierakonpolis—also provide strong evidence of the emergence of powerful rulers. A number of features depicted on prominent individuals, including scepters, crowns, kilts, penis sheaths, ostrich feathers, and a variety of weapons used in hunting and war, are all symbols of royal attire and power that were used by later pharaohs. Thus, it appears that many of the basic elements of kingship were already taking shape in Late Predynastic

The stone palette at right commemorates the victories of King Narmer, who has been credited with unifying Upper and Lower Egypt into a single state around 3050 B.C. In the top portion, the king's name is flanked by two bull's heads—symbols of pharaonic power. In the lower portion, Narmer inspects the decapitated bodies of his enemies.

times. The tombs also contain artifacts and depictions of weapons, particularly mace heads and knife handles, and display scenes of warfare in which the ruler is shown vanquishing enemies. The close association of royal symbols and warfare provides a clear indication of the role of militarism in the rise of regional chiefs.

In the final years of the Late Predynastic period, several large towns had emerged as centers of power in Lower and Upper Egypt. Each of these towns had its own patron deity, and each appears to have had administrative control over the surrounding countryside. In Lower Egypt, sizeable communities had grown up around Maadi, Heliopolis, Tarkhan, El-Omari, Helwan, Minshat, Tell Ibrahim Awad, and Pe. The latter appears to have been the major center, and eventually may have emerged as a regional capital of the delta region, perhaps even of all of Lower Egypt. In the north, Hierakonpolis, Naqada, and This were the major towns, and were likely the seats of power of chiefdoms or small kingdoms. These towns were at the top of a hierarchy of settlements in which village "chiefs" owed allegiance to district chiefs, who were in turn supporters of regional rulers. Thus an administrative hierarchy had emerged, that enabled paramount chiefs—or possibly kings—to manage the affairs of large regions. These local hierarchies eventually became the *nomes*, or administrative units, through which the pharaohs later governed the country. Nekhen, near Hierakonpolis, was the largest and wealthiest capital in Upper Egypt, and contained several clusters of mud-brick dwellings with plastered walls, numerous elite residences, cemeteries, and a core of public buildings. Its population, including the immediate surrounding region, is estimated to have reached 5000 to 10,000 people. Most scholars now agree that it eventually came to be the capital of an Upper Egyptian state or proto-kingdom by 3200 B.C. Pottery from the Gerzean period (the final Predynastic period of Upper Egypt) is found all along the Nile Valley, and as far away as the delta. This and other evidence suggest that Upper Egypt had gained the ascendancy in the final years of the Prepharaonic period.

EARLY DYNASTIC AND OLD KINGDOM PERIODS (3050 B.C. TO 2160 B.C.)

According to historic texts, Upper and Lower Egypt were unified into a single state through a series of conquests by the Pharaoh Narmer of Hierakonpolis sometime around 3050 B.C. This was a remarkable achievement, and created the largest state of its size in the world at that time; by comparison, the city-states of Mesopotamia controlled much smaller territories. Herodotus tells us that Narmer moved his capital to the north, where he founded a city known as "White Walls" (later known as Memphis) and established the First Dynasty. It is possible that this move was facilitated by Narmer's marriage to a daughter of one of the rulers of Lower Egypt. Several of his successors in the north married into southern ruling families as a way of maintaining control between Upper and Lower Egypt. This pattern of intermarriage appears to have been a key factor in the unification of the state. Narmer's successors consolidated their rule over the entire Nile Valley from the Mediterranean to Aswan. They also extended their control over the Western Desert, and sent expeditions into the Sinai to safeguard sources of copper and the trade routes to the Levant.

The legacy of the kings of the first two dynasties (3050 B.C. to 2695 B.C.) is largely found in a series of spectacular tombs at the site of Abydos, which was excavated by Petrie in 1902 and 1903. These structures, known as *mastaba* tombs, contained an underground compartment with a main burial chamber and adjoining rooms for the king's possessions. Above all of this was a rectangular superstructure resembling a royal palace enclosed by walls. The superstructure, which had an exterior made of brightly painted mud-brick panels, enclosed several courtyards and rooms containing all the necessities for living in the afterlife. Beyond the enclosure were rows of less elaborate tombs, for members of the royal entourage, wives, minor court functionaries, retainers, and servants, the last of whom were buried along with their owner, and whom they would continue to serve in the afterlife. Needless to say, Egyptian kings were undoubtedly well cared for during their mortal lives—after all, the servants had a vested interest in the good health of their masters; even the slightest illness would have been a source of major concern around the palace. These tombs, and those of later kings and nobles, had an unmistakable "residential" quality to them, which is not surprising, since they were to be the final dwelling place of the rulers throughout eternity. In contrast to contemporary practice and belief, the Egyptian elite did, in fact, take it all with them. As we shall see, this royal concern with the afterlife, which grew out of the funerary cult of Predynastic times, was to be a central focus of life in ancient Egypt.

This focus lies at the heart of the first cities of Egypt, many of which were literally built up around royal funerary monuments. This is why they have often been called temple towns. As noted, this temple focus once created the impression that the early towns of Egypt were primarily the site of temples and monuments, surrounded by the palaces of the pharaohs and the nobility and their retainers. Laborers, craftsmen, and farmers lived in nearby villages. Thus early Egypt was seen as a non-urban state. This view was at variance with the general model of the state proposed by Childe and other scholars, in which densely populated cities were an essential characteristic of state-level societies.

The lack of detailed settlement-pattern data has been a major part of the problem. In the course of many decades of palace archaeology, in which most excavations focused on monumental architecture, little or no work was carried out in the surrounding areas. As a result, we have limited information on the residential sectors of most Early Dynastic and Old Kingdom communities. Moreover, the residential areas of many early Egyptian cities—largely made of perishable mud-brick and plaster structures—have been destroyed or buried beneath the constructions of later periods. The annual flooding of the Nile washed out many early communities, depositing tons of silt on the remaining foundations; shifting desert sands have further obliterated traces of their remains.

To make matters worse, we know from historical records and observations made over the last two centuries that the remains of early settlements have been systematically destroyed by workers who used the materials to build later settlements or by farmers who dug up decayed brick for use as fertilizer. Needless to say, the settlements of the Early Dynastic and Old Kingdom periods have suffered the most from these destructive processes.

Studies conducted in the last three decades have nonetheless managed to piece together a broader perspective on these early communities. From historical texts and a growing body of recent archaeological evidence, we know that the Egyptian temple towns were more complex, more extensive, and more heavily populated than originally thought. Most scholars agree that while the major early Dynastic communities were not as densely populated as contemporary Mesopotamian cities, they were still fully urban in character.

The smaller size of the earliest cities of Egypt is in part determined by the Nile, as is so much of the course of Egyptian civilization. Settlers along the Nile favored a dispersed linear settlement pattern, because the narrow confines of the valley floodplain placed constraints on the number of people who could farm and live at any given location along the river. Archaeologist Fekri Hassan, who has conducted detailed subsistence and demographic studies of the floodplain, has convincingly argued that the agricultural carrying capacity (or its potential food production) "would hardly have been sufficient to support a burgeoning city and its hinterland." He goes on to observe that these limitations have been overcome in modern times with the development of more sophisticated irrigation and land reclamation projects and by improvements in agricultural technology and transportation.

Despite these early limitations, urban settlements developed at a number of locations along the upper and lower sections of the Nile Valley. Among the more prominent were Pe and Mendes in the delta; Heliopolis, Giza, Dahshur, and Memphis in Lower Egypt; and This, Nagada, Nekhen (Hierakonpolis), and Elephantine in Upper Egypt.

Given the lack of settlement-pattern data, it is difficult to discuss city planning in any detail. In fact, we do not have detailed plans of any Early Dynastic or Old Kingdom cities. Still, from historical and archaeological data we can discern a few general patterns. Most cities were laid out in linear fashion along the Nile, and built around, or adjacent to, the funerary core, which generally had a highly symmetrical plan set on a north-south axis. In some instances, the funerary core lay outside the city proper; or, to be more precise, the city grew outward from the core. The city itself displayed less evidence of planning because it grew in gradual stages. Typically, there were one or more major thoroughfares, from which smaller streets and winding alleys led into the various neighborhoods. At the heart of most cities was the royal compound, or funerary core, which included pyramids, tombs, mortuary temples, and palaces, often set in walled enclosures. Nearby lay the palaces of the nobility and the houses of government officials, bureaucrats, merchants, and master craftsmen. There are few remains of these early elite residences, but if those from later times are an indication, they were probably quite elaborate, multiroomed structures, with one or more stories, located around elegant courtyards and gardens. The walls of the rooms and courtyards were often painted with scenes of everyday life, with farming and hunting the main themes. In some cities, there were industrial and commercial sectors, containing workshops, storage areas, and markets and bazaars. Some cities, such as Memphis, had extensive port facilities, including wharves and warehouses. Beyond the city, sometimes set apart from it by a wall, lay the residential areas of the commoners. Many of these residential quarters were constructed as specially planned villages for the laborers who built the funerary monuments; later, they were inhabited by farmers, craftsmen, and workers in other professions. The dwellings of the commoners were simple, rectangular, mud-brick structures, set close together in tightly adjoining clusters. Cemeteries for the general population have been located at several towns; the king's retinue was generally buried in tombs surrounding the royal necropolis, as were members of the nobility.

The development of the early Egyptian city was closely tied to the rise of the institution of kingship. Royal power increased dramatically in the early dynasties, and a cult centered on the person of the pharaoh came into being, culminating in his acquisition of semi-divine status. An elaborate priesthood and a standing army were created, which answered only to him, thus guaranteeing his absolute power over all temporal and spiritual affairs. At the same time, the bureaucratic apparatus that was to govern Egypt for the next 3000 years emerged. At the pinnacle of the bureaucracy was the grand vizier, the supreme administrator of the state. Below him was a large hierarchy of palace officials, priests, military officials, scribes, tax

An important administrative and religious center grew up in the Early Dynastic period at Elephantine (modern-day Aswan), just north of the First Cataract on the Upper Nile.

collectors, census takers, architects and engineers, managers of irrigation systems, and minor clerics. Beyond the capital were the regional governors, who were the administrators of the nomes, and their respective underlings. Like our own civil service, this bureaucracy was ultimately stronger than the pharaoh himself; it would survive palace intrigues, revolts, even invasions, up until Roman times.

The rise of the state fostered a host of major innovations in the arts and sciences. Foremost among these was the development of hieroglyphic writing, a script that combined pictographic and phonetic elements. The concept of writing may have been introduced by traders from southwest Asia, but the script developed by Egyptian priests and scribes was markedly different. It may have been derived from motifs and designs used on Predynastic funeral pottery, but the new script also used a different medium—namely ink written on papyrus-reed paper—rather than clay tablets, although hieroglyphic texts were also inscribed on stone palettes and on monuments. As in Mesopotamia, the earliest texts were devoted primarily to economic transactions and record-keeping, which were an indispensable tool in the administrative affairs of the state. Later writings included historical accounts, administrative, economic, and legal documents, religious and medical texts, hymns, literary works, and scientific records.

As the power of the king increased, so did the scale of his funerary monuments. At the beginning of the Third Dynasty (about 2680 B.C.), Imhotep, the Grand Vizier and chief architect of King Djoser, designed a new kind of tomb

A six-stepped pyramid dominates the burial complex of King Djoser, at Saqqara, near Memphis, Egypt. Built about 2680 B.C. by Imhotep, the king's chief architect, it is the oldest known pyramid in the world.

for his master. At Saqqara, south of Cairo, they built what was essentially a mastaba tomb with a stepped pyramid erected on top. The pyramid of Djoser is the oldest known pyramid in the world.

True pyramids evolved relatively quickly, and became the hallmark of the Old Kingdom (2695 B.C. to 2160 B.C.). Much of the transition took place during the Fourth Dynasty (2613 B.C. to 2494 B.C.). At Meidum and Dahshur, two early pyramids were originally built as stepped structures, but then were covered over with a limestone facing that gave each the appearance of a "true" pyramid. Later, King Seneferu built the oldest "true" pyramid at Dahshur. Instead of a stepped core, the stones beneath the outer casing were laid in level courses from the ground up. The smooth outer casing of most pyramids, now mostly gone, was made of polished limestone. The burial chambers were generally located at or below the base of the pyramid, near its center, and were reached by a passageway from the outside. In some instances, as at the Great Pyramid at Giza, the King and Queen's burial chambers were located higher up within the pyramid.

The pyramid built by King Seneferu at Dahshur, Egypt, was the first to be built with level courses rather than stepped stages. During its construction, the angle of rise was considered too steep, so adjustments were made to change it from 54.5° to 43.5°, thus giving the structure its unusual "bent" profile.

As time went on, pyramids also became taller and steeper: the sides of Seneferu's true pyramid incline at an angle of 43° rather than the 52° angle that characterizes later pyramids. The most imposing of all of these monuments are the three pyramids of Giza, also built during the Fourth Dynasty. The largest of these, built by King Khufu (Cheops), covers 13 acres (5.3 hectares); all four sides of its base measure 754 feet (230 meters) in length, and the structure is more than 481 feet (146 meters) high. It contains more than two million stones, each weighing an average of 2.5 tons. Built around 2600 B.C., the Great Pyramid is generally acknowledged to be the largest structure in the ancient world. Petrie, who surveyed Giza in the 1880s, located the workers' village next to the pyramids, and estimated the ancient work force to have numbered some 4000 individuals. Most of the pyramids were built between the Third and Sixth Dynasties. Then, 200 years after the monuments of Giza were erected, the construction of large pyramids came to a halt. The reason for this is not known, though it is widely suspected that the megalomanical construction of royal monuments may have taken a heavy toll on the social system, forcing later monarchs to divert their labor surpluses into different, and less costly, public works.

Giza is perhaps the most majestic of the Old Kingdom cities, and is famous not only for its pyramids, but for other monuments as well. The most spectacular of these is the Great Sphinx, which has a human head placed on the body of a lion. The head is a likeness of King Khafre (Chephren), a successor of Cheops, who built the second-largest pyramid at Giza. Carved out of a rocky knoll, the Sphinx is 240 feet (73 meters) long; the head is more than 65 feet (20 meters) tall. It is believed to be a representation of the king as the Sun God, protecting the royal cemetery. Surrounding the large pyramids are several smaller pyramids and

The pyramids at Giza, the most remarkable structures of the Old Kingdom, were built during the Fourth Dynasty. From front to back, the three Great Pyramids are those of the pharaohs Menkaura (Mycerinus), Khafre (Chephren), and Khufu (Cheops). In the foreground are three smaller pyramids of queens.

mortuary temples, and a large royal necropolis for the nobility, priests, and high government officials. The elaborate mortuary temple of Khafre (Chephren), which lies in front of his pyramid, is linked by a 1700-foot-long (530-meter-long) causeway to a second temple complex, known as a valley temple, where funerary rites were also performed. Part of the rituals involved the use of funerary boats, five of which have been uncovered at this complex. The Great Sphinx also forms part of this valley temple complex. These causeway extensions from the main pyramid to a valley temple have been found at other sites as well; in some cases, the satellite temple was built at the edge of the Nile.

Another valley temple at Giza, originally built to accompany the pyramid of King Menkaura (Mycerinus), also lay at the end of a causeway almost 2000 feet (600 meters) long. The temple was a palatial structure, with a niched courtyard surrounded by several complexes of rooms and a sanctuary. In the three centuries that followed its construction, the courtyard and surrounding rooms were filled in with houses and silos for storing grain, transforming the structure into a self-contained, fortified village. Also at Giza is the funerary town associated with the tomb of Queen Khentkawes, also of the Fourth Dynasty. This complex was excavated by Egyptian archaeologist Selim Hassan in 1931 and 1932. The tomb itself is built around a large rectangular block of rock, to which a large masonry structure has been added; the mortuary temple is carved out of the eastern face of the rock. In front of it is a long row of buildings, laid out in an L-shaped plan. Most of these appear to be houses, connected by corridors. Each has a central room, two or three secondary rooms, a kitchen, and, in some instances, grain storage bins. Sometimes the mortuary temple itself included a residential sector. Such is the case at Abusir, where an enormous mortuary temple lies next to the pyramid of King Nefirirkara, a Fifth Dynasty ruler. At the heart of this complex is a large courtyard and a temple, set at the base of the pyramid. Flanking two sides of the courtyard are nine buildings of two to three rooms each, which were presumably houses. It is not clear who lived in these temple compounds, but it is possible that they were the dwellings of the rulers and their families and retainers, and, subsequently, of their descendants, who maintained the cult of the ruler long after his death.

The Early Dynastic and Old Kingdom periods encompass only the first 10 centuries of Egyptian history. The civilization of the Nile would continue, ruled by 23 later dynasties, for another 2000 years until it was conquered by a succession of Persian, Greek, and Roman rulers. Following the Old Kingdom, Egyptian rulers confronted numerous periods of instability, including revolts and invasions. There were also times of renewed grandeur, when new cities and grandiose monuments were built. One such period was that of the New Kingdom (1540 B.C. to 1070 B.C.), whose rulers included Akhenaton and Ramses II. The later periods would also see larger and more complex cities, such as Memphis, Kahun, El-Amarna, and Thebes. Still, much of the legacy of ancient Egypt was forged in the achievements of the Early Dynastic and Old Kingdom periods, which saw the rise of the state and the emergence of the first cities. In light of these accomplishments, many historians have referred to the Old Kingdom as Egypt's "Golden Age".

THE RISE OF THE EGYPTIAN STATE

While scholars might debate whether the first Egyptian state arose during Predynastic or Early Dynastic times, it was not until after the unification of Upper and Lower Egypt that most of the features of a true state apparatus came together. These include urban centers, legitimized kingship, a bureaucracy, taxation,

Bearing the scars of centuries of erosion, the Great Sphinx still proudly guards the entrance to the valley temple of King Khafre. The human head rests on the body of a lion and may represent the king as the Sun God.

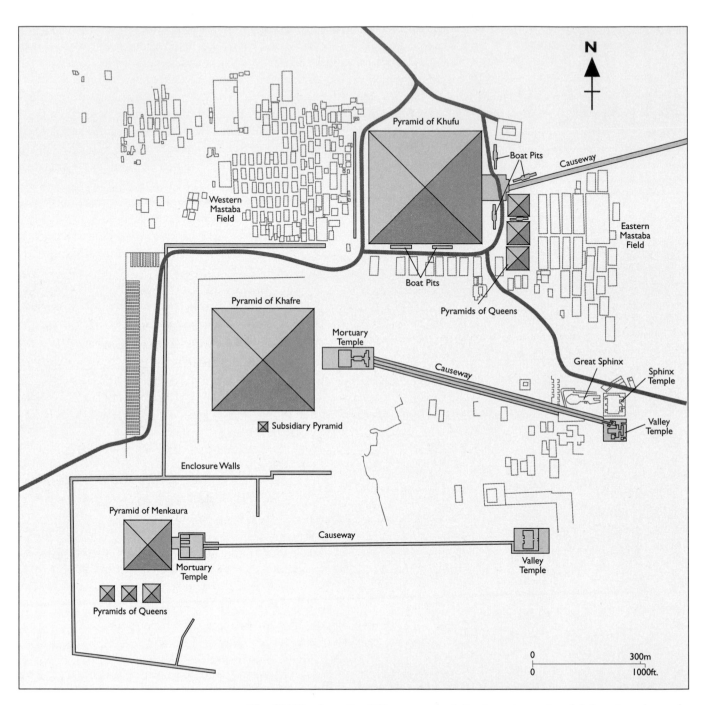

The Old Kingdom city of Giza was a carefully planned complex of shrines, temples, and causeways, each connected to one of the three Great Pyramids. Surrounding the royal cemetery is a large necropolis for the nobility, priests, and high officials. Recent excavations have also uncovered a large residential sector close to the Nile.

long-distance trade, a standing army, large public works, a unified monumental art style, and writing. Even though Egyptian cities were not densely populated, they were seats of administrative power, and the nerve centers for the socioeconomic and religious infrastructure that dominated Egypt. Many of the factors that gave rise to the Egyptian state can be traced to Predynastic times. Several scholars, most notably archaeologists Karl Butzer and Fekri Hassan, have proposed that the agricultural adaptation to the ecological conditions of the Nile was the main building block. Butzer has convincingly argued that the ups and downs of Egyptian civilization can be traced to successful or unsuccessful adaptations to fluctuating ecological conditions along the Nile, and the management of agricultural and labor surpluses in the face of those conditions. While population pressure and state management of irrigation systems do not seem to have made a major contribution to the rise of a complex society in Predynastic times, the effective management of agricultural production from early on was nonetheless critical. A key factor in the development of local power structures may have been the emergence of regional chiefs, who could manage the food production of large areas, thus overcoming shortages in areas flooded by the Nile with surpluses from other areas. This was especially true in Upper Egypt, where a narrower floodplain required a more integrated economy. The successful creation of such an economy provided southern rulers a greater degree of authority and legitimization, which in turn allowed them to gain ascendancy over the towns of the north. Once this was established, the next logical step was to take over the rich granaries of Lower Egypt, which led to the consolidation of the state.

The Egyptians themselves have identified warfare as the most important factor in the rise of the Egyptian state. War was a key instrument in the unification of Egypt, and would continue to play a major role throughout its history. The pharaohs maintained standing armies from Early Dynastic times onward, and a system of forts was built along the Nile to reinforce local administrative centers. Religion further enhanced the status of the ruler through the institution of divine kingship, which provided the ultimate legitimization of his power. Finally, the emergence of a bureaucracy reinforced and maintained the religious and military pillars of the state.

Other factors were also at work. The growing power of regional rulers and the emergence of a high-status funerary cult created a demand for luxury goods that accelerated the growth of craft specialization and production, thereby contributing to social differentiation. The demand for luxury goods also fueled long-distance trade, which was greatly aided by the development of effective water transportation. Trade itself played an important role, not only in unifying the economies of Upper and Lower Egypt, but also in providing a medium for the diffusion of ideas, including metallurgy and writing, from distant areas of the Near East.

The ancient city of Mohenjo-Daro lies some 200 miles (320 kilometers) north of Karachi, Pakistan. The labyrinth of eroded walls in the background
planned residences. Mohenjo-Daro and its sister city, Harappa, were the first and largest sites to be excavated of what has come to be known

4

THE INDUS: HARAPPAN CIVILIZATION

Most scholars wince at the idea of a "lost civilization" for the simple reason that civilizations rarely get lost. One exception is the Harappan culture, which literally was "discovered" by Sir John Marshall in 1921. While local people knew of the existence of scattered ruins along the shores of the Indus River in what is now Pakistan, no one suspected that the ruins were the remains of one of the world's oldest civilizations. But, in 1921, Marshall, then Director General of Archaeology in India, excavated two

was once part of a network of meticulously as the Harappan civilization.

of the largest archaeological sites in the Indus Valley, which were located 400 miles (640 kilometers) apart. The excavations led him to realize that Harappa and Mohenjo-Daro were complex, early Bronze Age urban sites belonging to the same culture, and were therefore contemporary with the ancient civilizations of Mesopotamia and Egypt. The announcement of this discovery, in a short article published in the *Illustrated London News* in 1924, caused quite a stir in scientific circles.

In the 1920s and 1930s, excavations were continued at both sites by a number of British and Indian scholars, including Marshall, E.J.H. Mackay, D.R. Sahni, M.S. Vats, and K.N. Sastri. Following World War II, Sir Mortimer Wheeler and several Pakistani colleagues conducted further excavations, which were continued in the 1960s by George Dales and others. Since then, there has been a tremendous surge of work throughout the Indus area by Pakistani, Indian, and foreign scholars.

As in the case of Egypt, it was originally thought that Harappan civilization had appeared practically overnight. The early recovery at Harappan sites of a

The Indus civilization developed along the valley of the Indus River, which snakes through Pakistan from its source in the Himalayas and empties into the Arabian Sea. A second river, the Ghaggar-Hakra—now dry—once also watered the Indus plain.

60

The lower reaches of the Indus River are located in the Sind region. The climate in this area is dry, so agriculture is limited to the river's floodplain. When the Indus reaches its delta, it breaks up into a multitude of small channels, like the one shown here, with extensive marshlands and lagoons near the sea.

few trade items from the Near East led many scholars to jump to the assumption that the Indus civilization was an offshoot of ancient Sumer. It has taken many years to dispel these notions. While the rise of cities appears to have taken place relatively rapidly in the Indus region—over a 100- to 150-year period—it was primarily the outcome of indigenous developments, rather than external influences. Trade with Iran and Mesopotamia was an important part of the Harappan economy, and may have played a significant role in the development of its cities, yet trade was only one of many factors that led to the rise of the highly unique civilization of the Indus.

The homeland of the Indus civilization extends like a cone out of northeast Pakistan, stretching down the Indus Valley to its delta on the Arabian Sea; near the sea, it extends westward along the Makran coast of southwest Pakistan and southeastward down the coast of northwest India to the Gulf of Cambay. The Indus plain originally included two major rivers, the Indus and the Ghaggar-Hakra, but the latter is now dry. The overall area's northeast-to-southwest axis extends about 1000 miles (1600 kilometers), while its seaboard extends some 750 miles (1200 kilometers).

The Indus region is made up of several major ecological areas. The northernmost area, where the site of Harappa lies, is known as the Punjab. This highland area, fed by the upper tributaries of the Indus, has high rainfall and fertile soils, and is a rich agricultural zone. The area to the south, known as the Sind, contains the Indus alluvial plain and the southern city of Mohenjo-Daro; the region is arid so that any land dedicated to cultivation is restricted to small, irrigated areas along the river bottomlands. The third major area is the delta, which is made up mostly of marshes and lagoons, through which the Indus

River channels empty into the sea. To the west of the delta lies the mountainous Makran coast; its southeast portion embraces the Bay and Island of Kush, the peninsula of Saurashtra, the Gujarat Plain, and the Gulf of Cambay.

EARLY FOOD-PRODUCING ERA

The oldest known villages in the Indus region appeared around 6500 B.C., at the dawn of what is called the Neolithic era (circa 6500 B.C. to 5000 B.C.). This early period is best known from excavations at a group of simple farming villages near Mehrgarh, 125 miles (200 kilometers) north of Mohenjo-Daro. These sites were excavated by the French archaeologist J-F. Jarrige and his colleagues in the 1970s.

The earliest communities of Mehrgarh consisted of small clusters of mud-brick, multiroomed structures that included hearths and/or ovens. These probably served both as houses and granaries. The presence of domesticated wheat and barley in the earliest levels of these communities suggests that the Indus was an independent center of plant domestication. Later domesticates of the Indus region included rice, millet, dates, peas, lentils, and cotton, the last of which the peoples of the Indus were among the first in the world to cultivate. This early farming economy was originally supplemented by hunting, as indicated by the remains of gazelle, antelope, onager, elephant, and several species of deer, as well as by those of wild species of sheep, goat, cattle, pig, and water buffalo. Towards the end of the early food-producing period, hunting was gradually replaced by a more pastoral economy, as most of the animal population consisted of domesticated sheep, goat, and cattle.

In the open areas adjoining the houses, several brick-lined burials have been uncovered. The contents of these burials offer a glimpse into the daily lives of these early settlers. Stone tools used in domestic activities, farming, and hunting were common, as were baskets covered with bitumen, which served as containers in lieu of pottery. Ceramics did not appear until the end of the period, around 5000 B.C. Several artifacts indicate a level of material culture and trading activity that is somewhat advanced for a simple farming society. These items included beads made from turquoise and lapis lazuli (traded from Iran and Afghanistan), shells from the Arabian Sea, a copper bead, and a lead pendant. The latter two items are quite rare, as metal artifacts do not become widespread until after 4000 B.C.

REGIONALIZATION ERA

Lasting roughly from about 5000 B.C. to 2600 B.C., the period called the Regionalization Era encompasses a long sequence of developments that archaeologists have labeled as Late Neolithic, Chalcolithic, Pre-Urban, Pre- or Early Harappan, or Early Indus. The main development during this period was the spread of a village-farming/pastoral way of life throughout the Indus basin. By 4000 B.C., settlements had appeared all along the alluvial plains.

These possessed a full complement of domesticated plants and animals, stone tools, grinding stones for processing food, and a variety of ceramic types, ranging from coarse handmade vessels for everyday use to fancier burnished, incised, and painted wares made on a simple turntable or wheel.

Most of the settlements were small farming villages with houses, though a few were larger. Gregory Possehl, who has conducted extensive research on the development of Harappan civilization, reports that during the final centuries of this period (3200 B.C. to 2600 B.C.) there were more than 460 settlements. The majority covered less than 10 acres (4 hectares) in area, although a few were as large as 25 acres (10 hectares), and at least three ranged between 54 and 74 acres (22 and 30 hectares). Among the larger and better known settlements are Harappa, Kalibangan, and Rahman Dheri in the northeast, Mehrgarh and Naushapo in the northwest, and Mohenjo-Daro, Kot Diji, Amri, and Balakot in the south. Most of the construction at these and other large sites appears to be residential in nature, consisting mostly of rectilinear buildings made of mud-brick or stone. While most of these were houses, some buildings evidently functioned as granaries, and a few may have been the locale of specialized craft activities, such as the making of pottery and the smelting of metal ores. At many sites there are irregular networks of streets and alleys, as well as drains and wells, indicating a moderate degree of community planning.

Monumental public works are relatively rare. Massive mud-brick platforms are found at a handful of sites, and large walls surround the settlements at Kalibangan, Kot Diji, and Kohtras Buthi. It has been suggested that the walls functioned as defensive fortifications, though they may have also provided protection from flooding or served administrative or ritual purposes. The available data suggests that while many set tlements reveal evidence of communal organization and planning, only a handful had the resources to mobilize a sizeable labor force for the construction of large public edifices.

The production of craft goods blossomed during this period, as craftsmen produced a wide range of goods made from clay, stone, copper, shell, and a variety of exotic stones, such as lapis lazuli, turquoise, agate, jasper, serpentine, and steatite. Many of the exotic materials were imported from Iran and Afghanistan through the growing trade networks. There was considerable progress in metallurgy, and a whole hierarchy of miners, smelters, metalworkers, and traders of copper and bronze artifacts emerged.

Goods made from clay included ceramic vessels, seals, and figurines. Ceramic vessels were produced in a wide range of shapes, including bowls, jars,

Because statues of women found in the ruins vastly outnumber those of men, it is thought that the inhabitants of Mohenjo-Daro venerated a female deity. As with the terra-cotta head shown here, the female statues generally are adorned with lavish jewelry and elaborate head-dresses associated with deity attire.

plates, and a vessel with a stemmed base known as an "offering stand". These were decorated in a variety of ways, ranging from simple incising and burnishing to more elaborate monochrome, bichrome, and polychrome painting. Painted designs varied considerably, from simple linear bands and geometric patterns to detailed depictions of plants and animals. Some communities appear to have specialized in pottery-making, and supplied surrounding regions with everything from basic domestic containers to the more elaborate wares used in special social events, rituals, and burials. Terra-cotta figurines were also widely made, often depicting human males and females with elaborate hairdos, as well as several types of animals.

The first seals appeared in the fourth millennium, and were made from clay, stone, and bone. The earliest ones were small flat disks known as "button seals," and were impressed on clay or bitumen, probably to indicate ownership of trade goods. Later types evolved into the finely carved stone seals of the Urban Harappan phase. While most of the early seal designs consisted of repetitive geometric motifs, some had abstract symbols that may have indicated a person's name, a vessel's contents, or some ritual event. Abstract symbols or

Cattle were domesticated sometime before 5000 B.C. in the Indus Valley, and soon became a mainstay of the Harappan economy. This small terra-cotta bull suggests the importance attached to cattle.

graffiti were also etched into the wet clay of ceramic vessels or other terra-cotta objects before firing. These symbols may have been the forerunners of the Indus script, which developed during the following period.

In reviewing the information we have on the Regionalization Era, which preceded the full-blown flowering of Indus civilization, archaeologists have yet to determine the full degree of complexity that had developed in the Indus culture prior to 2600 B.C. Unlike Mesopotamia, where we can document the gradual evolution of all the major features of a state-level society in late fourth millennium times, many aspects of the Indus culture remain obscure. On the one hand, we have a few sizeable settlements with a fair degree of internal organization and advanced levels of craft specialization and trade, suggesting a high degree of regional economic integration. Within these communities, there is some evidence for social stratification, in subtle differences in residential areas, and in uneven access to goods—the fancy pottery and exotic jewelry clearly reflect elite consumerism and control over the means of production and trade. On the other hand, we have yet to uncover ostentatious displays of social status, such as palatial residences, elaborate tombs, and monumental public works that would suggest the existence of a highly stratified society. Nor are there any telltale signs warfare and conquest, or even of political organization at the regional level, such as existed in Predynastic Egypt.

URBAN HARAPPAN PHASE

Towards the middle of the third millennium, in what is called the Integration Era (2600 B.C. to 2000 B.C.), the Indus region underwent a phenomenal period of growth that produced one of the most complex early civilizations in the world. Population growth was one of its most visible features, as is evident in the numbers and sizes of settlements throughout the Indus region. Gregory Possehl estimates that the number of settlements during this period more than doubled, to over 970. Several of the settlements reached the proportions of full cities, and exhibit tremendous diversity in their public and residential architecture. Archaeologist Mark Kenoyer has organized the settlements into a four-tiered hierarchy. The first tier consists of true cities, which included Harappa (370 acres, or 150 hectares), Mohenjo-Daro (variously reported as 309 to 494 acres, or 125 to 200 hectares), Ganwariwala (200 acres, or 80 hectares), and Rakhigarhi (198 acres, or 80 hectares). The first two were among the largest cities of the world at that time, and were rivaled only by Uruk in Mesopotamia. The second tier, which might be considered the equivalent of towns, range in size from 25 to 125 acres (10 to 50 hectares), and include Kalibangan, Dholavira, and Judeirjo-Daro. The third tier is made up of large villages 12 to 25 acres (5 to 10 hectares) in area, such as Amri, Lothal, Chanhu-Daro, and Rojdi. The fourth and lowest tier is made up of hundreds of villages covering less than 12 acres (5 hectares).

Several scholars have commented on the uniformity of Harappan civilization, and this is particularly evident in many of its urban centers and large

The Great Bath at Mohenjo-Daro, set among once stately public buildings, may have served both commoners and priests as a center for performing ritual ablutions. The bath was reached by a staircase at either end. Colonnades supported a roof that covered small rooms where, it is thought, dignitaries could take their baths in private.

towns, which display similar layouts and orientation. For example, at Harappa, Mohenjo-Daro, and Kalibangan, a citadel with a north-south axis placed on a high, mud-brick platform lies on the western side of the settlement, overlooking a lower town to the east, which housed the bulk of the population. The citadel was surrounded by massive walls, and, in some instances, the lower town was similarly fortified. Many cities and towns also had regular street grids oriented to the cardinal points, a fact that is frequently cited as the earliest evidence of urban planning in the world, and stands in marked contrast with the nucleated, organic growth of Mesopotamian cities. The main avenues were often twice the width of the secondary streets, and three or four times the width of the smaller lanes and alleys.

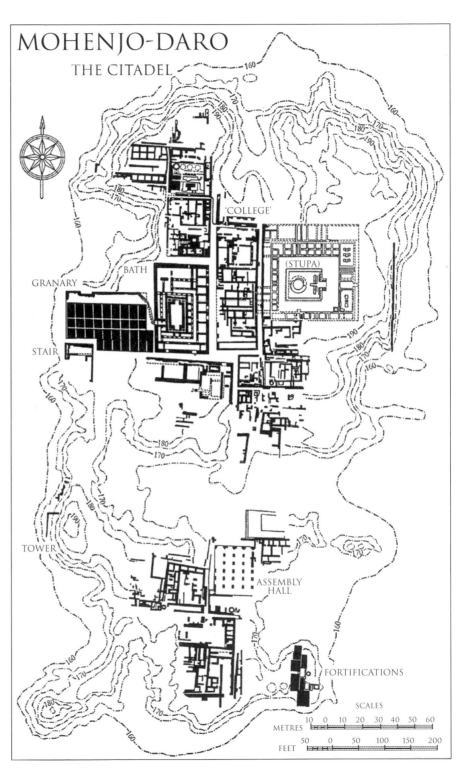

MOHENJO-DARO

THE CITADEL

'COLLEGE'

(STUPA)

BATH

GRANARY

STAIR

TOWER

ASSEMBLY
HALL

FORTIFICATIONS

SCALES

METRES 10 0 10 20 30 40 50 60

FEET 50 0 50 100 150 200

The regular layout of Mohenjo-Daro, like
other Harappan cities, is in marked contrast to the haphazard, nucleated growth
of Mesopotamian cities. The map at right
depicts the layout of the city's citadel.
The main residential areas of the city lay
to the east, and, like the citadel, were
oriented north-south.

Among the more prominent features of these cities were the extensive residential quarters, large state granaries, artisans' quarters and workshops, bazaars, public wells, cemeteries, and complex drainage systems designed to handle waste water and the periodic floods of the Indus River. The absence of royal tombs and clearly identifiable elite palaces and temples has posed a serious quandary to archaeologists. While many of the monumental buildings in the citadels at Harappa and Mohenjo-Daro may have served as palaces, administrative complexes, and temples, we have no hard evidence of the activities that took place in these precincts. This lack of information may be partly due to disturbances that took place in later periods, which obscured the original functions of the buildings. It is difficult to conceive that such a highly organized society would not have had a prominent ruling class with the usual trappings of wealth and power. Alternatively, we are left with the notion that the Indus elite may have had different values from those of other early urban societies and were perhaps less concerned with conspicuous displays of wealth and power.

The remains of a Buddhist stupa rise from a tumulus at the western edge of Mohenjo-Daro. It is thought that a rectangular platform, possibly the city's main temple from its earliest building phase, was covered over by the stupa, which is dated to the third or fourth century A.D.

Wheat and barley were major staples of Harappan civilization. Raised threshing platforms like the examples shown here—excavated at Harappa—were used to pound the grain harvest so as to separate the grain from the husks.

This 4.5-inch (11-centimeter) figurine of a dancing girl clad only in metal armlets and a necklace is one of the few bronze artifacts discovered at Mohenjo-Daro.

The southern city of Mohenjo-Daro is one of the finest monuments of the Indus civilization, and an excellent example of Harappan urbanism. The city is located in the Sind on the west bank of the Indus River, some 200 miles (320 kilometers) north of the modern-day port city of Karachi. The surrounding alluvial plains provided rich farmland for feeding the city. The city itself occupied an area of 309 to 494 acres (125 to 200 hectares). At its height, Mohenjo-Daro is estimated to have had a population of some 40,000 people. The city's most imposing feature is its citadel, which is laid out on a north-south axis atop an enormous, rectangular, mud-brick platform measuring roughly 650 by 1300 feet (200 by 400 meters), and rising about 40 feet (12 meters) above the floodplain. The massive walls that surround it include several towers, and may have served as fortifications and/or as protection against floods (excavations have revealed that the adjoining lower town was flooded on several occasions).

Most of the buildings in the north part of the citadel are laid out along a 30-foot-wide (9-meter-wide) north-south avenue. The most striking construction is a large sunken courtyard known as the Great Bath. It measures approximately 23 by 40 feet (7 by 12 meters), and is 8 feet (2.5 meters) deep. It is surrounded by colonnaded halls, and is flanked on the east by a row of eight small rooms. By analogy with later historic-period structures, it has been suggested, without much basis in fact, that this was a public ritual bathhouse, with the small rooms serving as private bathrooms.

Adjoining the Great Bath on its west side is the Granary, a rectangular structure that once supported a large building made of timber. Sir Mortimer Wheeler believed this to be a repository for storing grain, because of a grid of

underlying ducts that would have allowed air to circulate and prevented the grain from rotting. A similar structure has been uncovered at Harappa, and includes workers' quarters and several circular platforms used for pounding grain. It thus seems likely that these buildings served as state granaries, dedicated to the storage and preparation of the agricultural products of the surrounding lands.

Another large building to the northeast of the Granary, known as the College, consists of a large complex of rooms and courtyards, but its function eludes us. It has been suggested that it served as an administrative center, or as a residence for civil or religious authorities. It is the closest thing to a palace that has been found at the site. East of the College lie the remains of a stupa, or Buddhist shrine, built long after the Bronze Age. Some archaeologists believe that this may have been the site of Mohenjo-Daro's main temple, razed when the later shrine was built. In the southern part of the citadel lies another imposing building, known as the Assembly Hall. Ninety-two feet (28 meters) to a side, it houses 20 large pedestals, which likely served as bases for large wooden columns that probably supported a timber roof. While the conjecture that this served as a place for public assembly is a reasonable one, we have no idea what the purpose of such gatherings may have been.

The lower town of Mohenjo-Daro is laid out in a neat grid, with main streets oriented in a general north-south and east-west direction. These streets, which were unpaved, measured up to 32 feet (10 meters) in width, and included enclosed brick drains—the earliest such constructions in the world—that collected waste water from the houses. The city blocks, which measure approximately 820 by 1200 feet (250 by 370 meters), were subdivided into smaller units by alleys ranging from 5 to 10 feet (1.5 to 3 meters) in width. A particularly striking feature of the residential sector is the high quality of many of the individual homes. Many were two-storied, and centered around an open courtyard. The surrounding spacious rooms often included a bathroom, some with toilets, with a clay pipe leading to the street drain. Such amenities were undoubtedly unique in the early Bronze Age. Many houses had their own private wells, although communal wells were also found in the streets and neighborhood courtyards. Privacy seems to have been highly desired; the main entrances of the homes—designed in such a way as to prevent passersby from seeing inside the house—opened onto the side alleys, and windows are rare. Such elegant abodes are a good measure of the wealth of a large portion of the city's inhabitants. There are also, of course, remains of the houses of the lower classes, as well as several buildings that appear to have been barracks or slave quarters. In addition, there are a number of buildings whose functions have not been determined. Some of these may have been artisan workshops, and it has been suggested that at least one building may have been a temple or shrine; however, there is little evidence to support this notion.

One of the hallmarks of the Indus civilization is the high quality of its craft production. Among the more prominent products were painted pottery, inlaid woodwork, shell artifacts, beads of long carnelian, agate, turquoise, and lapis

Seals carved on steatite or crafted from metal are thought to have been a means of identifying personal property. The third-millennium terra-cotta seal shown here depicts a Brahma bull, with its characteristic hump and neck folds clearly defined. This species is held sacred today in India, and also may have been revered in Mohenjo-Daro.

lazuli, stoneware bangles, steatite seals, and a variety of objects made from copper, bronze, silver, and gold. The metalworkers, familiar with the processes of smelting, alloying, and casting, produced a diverse range of tools, weapons, vessels, ornaments, and figurines of humans and animals. There is a high level of standardization in Indus crafts, which may be due to the fact that many items were produced by communities that specialized in certain types of craft goods. Many settlements made pottery and metal artifacts: Chanhu-Daro manufactured long carnelian beads, shell ladles, and steatite beads; Shortugai, a Harappan trading post in northern Afghanistan, was a major center for the mining and production of lapis lazuli artifacts; stone bangles were manufactured at Mohenjo-Daro and Harappa; and shell artifacts were produced at the coastal towns of Nageshwar and Balakot. Moreover, it is possible that many goods were produced at these locations by kin-related craftspeople, which would further explain the high degree of standardization. The production of certain goods, especially those requiring the import of raw materials from distant sources, may have been controlled by the state, but this has yet to be verified.

There are several lines of evidence attesting to the existence of a highly integrated system of exchange in the Indus region. Foremost is the wide distribution of goods made from raw materials coming from limited source areas. Lapis lazuli is found only in Afghanistan, shells come from the coasts, and many varieties of certain minerals, such as agate (the source of carnelian), jasper, and red sandstone come from specific source areas. Also, the widespread use of clay sealings throughout the region—on storage vessels and packages of certain products—is indicative of widespread trade. However, the most compelling evidence of an organized trading system are the famous weights and measuring devices found at many Indus sites. The weights consist of standardized cubes of multicolored stone (generally chert), and range in size from .03 to 380 ounces (.9 to 10,865 grams). These were used with scales to weigh a wide range of goods, from spices to jewelry. The presence of these highly uniform weight cubes throughout the Indus region is unequivocal evidence of a tightly knit regional trading system. What is not known is whether such a formal system of weights was imposed and maintained by state authorities, or by common agreements among merchants.

Trade goods were transported in several ways. Overland trade traveled on ox-drawn carts and possibly on the backs of camels and elephants. The Indus was a major trade artery, and sailing craft—similar to modern Arab dhows—flowed from Harappa to the Arabian Sea and beyond, to India, Arabia, and the Persian Gulf.

Long-distance trade reached far and wide. As noted above, the Harappans set up a trading colony at Shortugai, in northeastern Afghanistan, to supply them with lapis lazuli, copper, and tin. The latter two metals were also brought in from Baluchistan, India, and possibly Oman, on the Arabian Peninsula. Gold came from southern India, and possibly also from Afghanistan. Silver was traded from Afghanistan or Iran, and lead from India. Central Asia was the source of several trade goods, including jade and turquoise. Turquoise also came from eastern Iran, which was a major source of steatite as well. Much of the overland trade to the west was by way of two major trade centers in eastern Iran, Tepe Yahya and Shahr-I-Sokhta. From these two towns, traders traveled as far as Susa in western Iran, and to the cities of Mesopotamia. Trade with Sumer was also carried by sea, by way of the Makran coast and the Persian Gulf. Although they are rare, Harappan artifacts—mostly seals, carnelian beads, and objects of lapis lazuli—have been recovered at Susa, Oman, Bahrain, and several Sumerian

A well-developed system of long-distance trade supplied the Indus cities with raw materials. Artisans fashioned these into the exquisite craft items that are among the hallmarks of Harappan civilization. From Afghanistan came lapis lazuli, copper, and tin. Ox-cart caravans brought turquoise from Iran, while sailing craft plied the seas between the Indus and trading cities in the Persian Gulf and along the shores of the Arabian Sea.

cities. Other Indus trade goods may have included copper, tin, ivory, and pearls. Moreover, Sumerian tablets refer to trading activities with Dilmun (Bahrain), Magan (Oman) and Meluhha (the Indus region), and to the presence of Meluhhan ships and traders in Sumerian cities. The trade from Sumer to the Indus is more difficult to document, as few Mesopotamian artifacts have been recovered at Harappan cities. It is possible that Sumerian imports may have been mostly perishable goods, such as textiles, timber, and spices.

As was the case in other Bronze Age civilizations, the Indus culture had a system of writing, although it remains largely undeciphered. Most scholars suspect that the Harappans spoke a proto-Dravidian language, but other languages may have been spoken in the Indus region as well. The Indus inscriptions, most of which are limited to five or six hieroglyphic signs, occur on seals and seal impressions, pottery stamps, small steatite and copper tablets, and as graffiti on pottery. The script consists of some 400 signs, and was neither alphabetic nor logographic (that is, having one character per word), but rather logo-syllabic, a system in which some characters represented words and others simple syllabic sounds. It was written from right to left; in rare instances where a text had more than one line, the second line was written from left to right, the third right to left, and so on. At present, the entire corpus of the script is limited to approximately 4000 inscriptions. Although decipherment has been slow, it appears that the script was used primarily for the purposes of identification (name, status, lineage, place, ownership), storage and accounting, and for recording economic transactions. Numerical signs consisted of vertical strokes for the numbers one through seven, and special symbols for numbers eight through ten; it was a base-eight system. Other inscriptions appear to record marriages (and alliances between different clans), while others identify chiefs and administrators; thus, some of the texts may contain political information.

We know next to nothing about Harappan religion. Since the excavations at Harappan cities have failed to identify any clearly identifiable examples of temples or royal burials, we have few hints as to Harappan views of the afterlife. Together with the lack of any textual information, this has seriously handicapped the study of the subject. There are, however, hints of ritual activity and beliefs. The Great Bath at Mohenjo-Daro has widely been interpreted as the locale for ritual ablutions. Burials in a cemetery at Harappa include a variety of ceramic vessels, personal ornaments, and toiletry items, suggesting at least a belief in the afterlife. Excavations have also yielded many clay female figurines—often depicted nude, sometimes pregnant, and sometimes with children—which have been interpreted as evidence of a fertility cult.

While the lack of royal palaces and tombs means there is scant evidence for a well-defined elite class, there is little question that Harappan society was strongly stratified. As several scholars have pointed out, there are numerous indicators of social differences. A well-defined hierarchy of settlements, ranging from simple farming communities to large cities with a prosperous "middle class," is perhaps the most basic of these. Moreover, there is considerable variation in domestic architecture within the larger communities, accompanied by evidence of occupational specialization and differential access to consumer goods. Given the substantial role of trade in Harappan culture, there is little doubt that merchants formed a prominent and wealthy socioeconomic class. The identification of "chiefs" in numerous inscriptions provides tentative evidence of an elite administrative class at the community and regional levels.

Beyond the scattered hints of the existence of regional elites, very little is known about Harappan political organization; no rulers have been identified, nor do we know what kind of government they had. While the cities clearly show a high degree of organization, undoubtedly managed by an administrative apparatus, we have no idea as to whether the region as a whole was made up of a group of independent polities, or whether it formed part of a single, centralized state. Early researchers speculated that Harappa and Mohenjo-Daro were the capitals of two independent but closely allied states, or joint capitals of the same state, but there is no conclusive proof for either scenario. On the other hand, the similarities in layout of several major cities, the state granaries, the shared religious motifs and architectural styles, the relatively uniform artistic corpus (which does exhibit some regional variation), the system of writing and standardized measures, and the highly integrated regional economy all suggest a degree of political unification generally associated with state-level societies. On this, most scholars would agree. Nonetheless, the nature of its political structure remains the single most elusive aspect of ancient Indus civilization.

POST-HARAPPAN PHASE

Sometime around 2000 B.C., at the beginning of what is called the Localization Era (1900 B.C. to 1300 B.C.) Harappan civilization went into a sharp decline. Many settlements, including Mohenjo-Daro, were abandoned. Other cities and towns, such as Harappa, continued to be inhabited, but monumental construction ceased, and many of the prosperous neighborhoods were invaded by squatters. A few settlements continued to grow, especially in the Gujarat region of northwest India, but they do not display many of the features that characterized high Harappan culture. In fact, they exhibit highly localized forms of construction, craft production, and socioeconomic integration. There is a pronounced decline in the uniformity of the culture, with the overall trend towards decentralization and regionalization. It has been suggested that this pattern may reflect a disintegration of centralized authority, as regional polities broke away and ceased to share a common ideological and economic system.

It is not clear what caused the disintegration of Harappan civilization. In the older literature, the Harappan decline is portrayed as a cataclysmic collapse, brought on by massive floods and invading hordes of Aryans from the north. While there is no evidence to support foreign invasions or sudden floods, it appears that environmental factors did play a role in the southern part of the Indus Basin. Sedimentation and tectonic uplift led to the drying-up of the Ghaggar-Hakra River, bringing about a disruption of agricultural systems and the abandonment of many communities along its course. Similar processes occurred along the Indus, which began to shift to the east, flooding many settlements. Still, these events did not have a major impact in the north, in the region around Harappa, and therefore cannot explain the decline of the entire system. It is also difficult to imagine that such a complex culture would not have adjusted to changes in the regional environment. Scholars therefore suspect that the reasons for the decline are far more complex, and will remain a challenging subject of research for many years to come.

THE RISE OF INDUS URBANISM

There are two schools of thought on the rise of urbanism in the Indus Valley. Between 2600 B.C. and 2500 B.C., one of these sees an abrupt transition from a relatively simple agricultural and pastoral society to a complex urban culture. In this scenario, the sudden flowering of Harappan high culture, which Gregory Possehl has called a "paroxysm of change," was heavily influenced by trade, which in turn led to major changes in craft production, social stratification, and ideology. It has been widely suggested in the literature that long-distance trade, especially with Iran and Mesopotamia, was a major factor in the rise of the Indus civilization. However, most of the evidence of heavy volume trade with the Persian Gulf area dates to after 2300 B.C., long after the emergence of the Harappan cities. On the other hand, there is substantial evidence of large-scale internal exchange and of external trade with adjoining regions—such as Iran, Afghanistan, and India—prior to 2500 B.C. There is little doubt that this trade played a significant role in the rise of complex social systems in the Indus region.

A second school suggests that the rise of urbanism was a more gradual process, an outgrowth of indigenous developments that began in the Pre-Urban phase of Harappan culture. Most scholars favor this line of thinking and do not see a sudden transition between the two periods. They argue instead that the region already shared a highly integrated socioeconomic system prior to 2600 B.C., and that the appearance of true cities and complex political organization was the natural outcome of local development.

The resolution of the differences between these two schools will lie in future research to determine just how much of a transition there was between the Pre-Urban and Urban phases of Harappan civilization, and how abrupt this change was. Trade and local development were undoubtedly both important in the rise of urbanism, but there were likely other forces at work. For example, there is almost no information on population pressure, warfare, political dynamics, or ideology—critical factors that shaped early urban societies elsewhere. Further excavations and decipherment of the Harappan script will surely shed new light on these processes, and lead to more encompassing explanations that will do justice to the complexity of Indus civilization.

Harvesting rice in China's southern Anhui Province goes on today much as it has for thousands of years. Since the beginning of civilization in China, domesticated in the southern and eastern regions of the country as early as 5000 B.C.

rice has been the main staple. The grain was

5

CHINA: SHANG CIVILIZATION

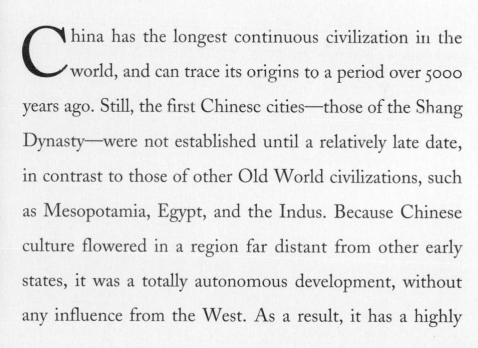

China has the longest continuous civilization in the world, and can trace its origins to a period over 5000 years ago. Still, the first Chinese cities—those of the Shang Dynasty—were not established until a relatively late date, in contrast to those of other Old World civilizations, such as Mesopotamia, Egypt, and the Indus. Because Chinese culture flowered in a region far distant from other early states, it was a totally autonomous development, without any influence from the West. As a result, it has a highly distinctive character. In China, as in other parts of the world, the culture developed out of a long, local Neolithic tradition, and its first cities did not appear until around 1500 B.C.

The study of the past has long been a central concern of Chinese scholars, and has its roots in an age-old tradition of historiography and antiquarianism going back several centuries before the Christian era. However, modern archaeology only began with the establishment of the Geological Survey of China in 1916. This was staffed by a number of Western scholars, including J. Gunnar Andersson, Davidson Black, Pierre Teilhard de Chardin, and Franz Weidenreich. These men exerted substantial influence on subsequent Chinese archaeology, and trained several students who later became prominent Chinese archaeologists. Their fieldwork involved extensive surveys of many regions of China, and preliminary excavations at a number of sites. Among their most prominent accomplishments—during the 1920s—was the discovery and excavation of the first Lower Paleolithic site in China, which contained the remains of *Homo erectus* ("Peking Man"), at the caves of Zhoukoudien, near Beijing, and the identification and excavation of the first Neolithic sites of the Yangshao culture of northern China. One Chinese scholar who participated in these excavations, Li Chi, eventually rose to become the father of Chinese archaeology. Chi completed his doctoral studies at Harvard, and went on to direct the

Pierre Teilhard de Chardin, shown at right above, was ordained as a Jesuit priest before becoming a paleontologist. His work with the Geological Survey of China in the 1920s and 1930s led to the discovery of the first remains of *Homo erectus* (subsequently referred to as "Peking Man"). At right is the excavation work underway at the Zhoukoudien Caves, near Beijing, where the discovery was made.

The earliest human settlements in China appeared in the south and east. However, it was in northern China—particularly in the valley of the Yellow River—that settled communities first evolved into true cities. With the rise of the Shang Dynasty in 1766 B.C., Chinese civilization came into full flower.

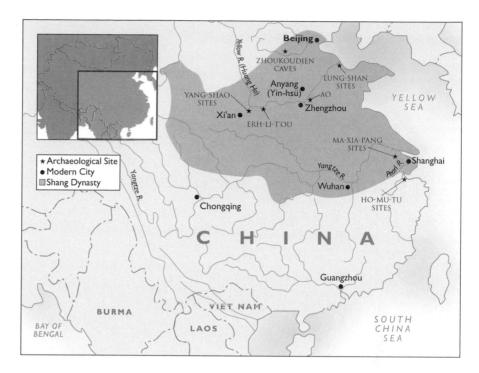

large-scale excavations of the Late Shang capital of Yin-hsü, where a whole generation of Chinese archaeologists was trained. In 1945, he was named director of the Central Historical Museum, and later established the first department of archaeology at the National Taiwan University in Taipei. Another major scholar of ancient Chinese studies was Kuo Mo-jo, a writer who began a series of studies of inscriptions on oracle bones and bronzes in the 1930s. This pioneer work paved the way for much of subsequent research on the early Chinese script, and led to Mo-jo's election as president of the Chinese Academy of Sciences in 1950, a post he held until his death in 1978. His representation of the Shang as a slave society set the tone for a whole generation of scholars who interpreted early Chinese civilization from a Marxist perspective, a trend that dominated the field for several decades. Contemporary Chinese archaeologists continue the research traditions established by Chi and Mo-jo, although the dogmatic Marxist research of recent times is giving way to more liberal trends. Most of Western knowledge about Chinese archaeology comes from the work of Kwang-chih Chang, who has been the foremost chronicler and theoretical scholar of the subject since the 1960s.

GEOGRAPHY AND ECOLOGY

China is a huge land, with a tremendous diversity in topography, climate, and vegetation. From the subarctic taiga of Manchuria and the deserts and steppes of Chinese Turkestan, the terrain gives way to the alluvial plains of the Yellow

(Huang Ho) River and the hilly country of the southeast, to the high plateaus of Tibet, and the tropical jungles of the southwest. The landscape is dominated by mountains and hills, and a series of west-east river valleys that flow into the Yellow and China seas. These valleys, with their rich agricultural soils, provided the setting for most of the early cultural developments.

China is generally divided into two main physiographic and cultural regions, known as the Northern and Southern deciduous zones. The north is further subdivided into the northern forests and steppes, and the Yellow River Valley and its tributaries. The Yellow River region includes the loess highlands of the west, the alluvial plains of the east, and the Shandong Peninsula on the coast of the Yellow Sea. Northern China has a temperate climate and limited rainfall, is semiarid, and was once covered with deciduous-coniferous forests.

The Southern Deciduous Zone is made up of a network of river systems, including the Yangtze, Huai, and Pearl; it also includes the Red Basin of Sichuan, the Yangtze-Huai plain, and many hilly areas and lake districts. It enjoys a subtropical climate, abundant rainfall, and both subtropical and tropical forests.

THE NEOLITHIC (7000 B.C. TO 3000 B.C.)

Two Neolithic traditions emerged in China, one in the north and the other in the south and east. The earliest known evidence of farming comes from the north, where remains of domesticated broom-corn and fox-tail millet, and of Chinese cabbage, have been recovered at sites dating between 6500 B.C. and 5500 B.C. In the south, the oldest grains of rice are dated to 5000 B.C. at several sites in the Middle and Lower Yangtze Valley. Rice agriculture became widespread throughout the south and east after 5000 B.C., and has been a major staple of Chinese civilization ever since. Few sites are known from before 5000 B.C., and they consist of cave sites and small hamlets. These sites have yielded a variety of stone and bone tools, some of which were employed in hunting and fishing, as well as grinding stones used to process plant foods. Animal remains include wild mammals, birds, reptiles, and fish, and, possibly, domesticated pig. The inhabitants also made a simple pottery, decorated with cord marks, punctuations, and incised crosshatching.

After 5000 B.C., a number of farming cultures appeared across southern China. Prominent among these was the Ma-xia-pang culture of the lower Yangtze River Valley. Here, in the Lake T'ai-hu region west of Shanghai, more than 100 early farming villages have been located, and several have been excavated. These people grew rice, bottle gourds, water chestnuts, and lotus seed; kept domesticated dogs, pigs, and water buffalo; collected shellfish; fished; and hunted a wide range of wild animals. They lived in rectangular houses made of timber, with reed and clay walls, floors made of packed sand, shell, and clay, and roofs of reeds, bamboo, and straw. They were skilled potters, and manufactured bowls and jars in a variety of shapes, many of which included pedestals, tripod feet, and handle lugs. The finest pottery was painted

With its source in northern China's Kunlun Mountains, the Yellow River flows through varied terrain before reaching the sea. Here, a broad expanse of the waterway cuts through the mountains of Gansu Province, near Lan-chou. It was in the fertile valley of the Yellow River, in the fifth millennium B.C., that the early agricultural settlements—later known as the Yang-shao culture—were established.

and decorated with incised designs, and often accompanied burials. Several cemeteries have been located at these sites, and the burials reflect a wide range in wealth, from those of rich individuals buried with ornate pottery and artifacts, to poorer ones interred with only a few shards.

Roughly contemporary to the Ma-xia-pang was the nearby southern Ho-mu-tu culture, which lay near the coast of Hang-chou Bay south of present-day Shanghai. These people also relied on a combination of farming, hunting, and fishing, and raised dogs, pigs, and water buffalo. They lived in large, rectangular timber houses built on timber pilings, and developed a rich material culture of decorated ceramics, stone and bone artifacts, and figurines of humans and animals made from clay, ivory, and wood.

In northern China, agriculture spread quickly after about 6000 B.C., and cultural developments soon overtook the south. Unlike the southerners, with their heavy reliance on rice, northern farmers domesticated other cereal crops. Several early villages in Henan Province, in the Yellow River Valley, have yielded evidence of the cultivation of broom-corn and fox-tail millet, as well as sorghum, by 5000 B.C. The most distinctive Neolithic development of northern China was the Yang-shao culture, of the Middle Yellow River Valley, which dates from 5000 B.C. to 3000 B.C. (in some areas it lasted even

PREVIOUS PAGE: **The people of the Yang-shao culture built their villages on high ground to avoid flooding, and busied themselves with a variety of tasks, as this illustration shows. They grew cereal crops and raised domesticated animals, including pigs, sheep, and goats. The culture's distinctive pottery, painted red with black designs, featured large storage jars, such as those placed in the storage pit in the foreground.**

longer). Named for the village where it was first discovered, in 1920, the Yang-shao culture is best known for its pottery, which was painted red with black designs, and for its polished stone axes and knives.

Yang-shao villages were moderate in size; the largest covered 12 to 15 acres (5 to 6 hectares). The villages were built on high ground to avoid flooding, and generally consisted of residential areas, kilns, and cemeteries. The semi-subterranean houses were built in a variety of shapes (round, square, rectangular or oblong), made of timber posts with wattle and daub (mud smeared over a framework of sticks), and thatched roofs. They often included hearths and storage pits, with animal pens nearby. The staple crop was fox-tail millet, although broom-corn millet was also farmed. Domesticated animals included dogs, pigs, and water buffalo, and, to a lesser extent, cattle, sheep, and goats. These farmers also raised silkworms, giving rise to an industry that was to remain exclusively Chinese for several millennia.

As in the south, the northern Chinese cultures also show signs of social differentiation, even at this early stage. The varying sizes of houses in the villages and the uneven distribution of burial goods clearly indicate differences in wealth, and presumably in social status as well.

While the societies of southern China continued to forge a prosperous farming way of life, after 3000 B.C. they were overshadowed by the more complex developments taking place in the north.

LUNG-SHAN CULTURES

In northern China, the first centuries of the third millennium saw significant advances in the farming societies of the Yellow River Valley, known collectively as the Lung-shan cultures (3000 B.C. to 1766 B.C.). The population grew substantially as the number of communities multiplied. Many settlements grew into what we would today call towns, and were often surrounded by large earthen walls, built to protect against flooding and attacks by raiders. These increasingly complex communities were to form the backbone of later Shang civilization.

Perhaps the most important development in this period was the adoption of rice cultivation, which was introduced from the warmer and wetter regions of the south. The adoption of rice in many dry areas was made easier by the development of irrigation systems. More importantly, the introduction of rice reduced dependency on cereal crops, hunting, and gathering, and produced a more diversified agricultural base. The surplus provided by this expanded agricultural base probably encouraged the growth of population as well as the increased level of social complexity that characterized the flourishing communities of the Lung-shan era.

Perhaps the best evidence for this growing social complexity is the appearance of widespread craft specialization throughout northern China. Lung-shan pottery-making surpassed that of earlier periods. The pottery was made both

As long ago as the fourth millennium B.C., the Chinese believed that spirits resided in bones, and that through them the future could be foretold. A diviner would examine the patterns of cracks that was created by the application of heat to a specially treated bone, such as this ox scapula; he would then read the answers to specific questions that had been written on the bone.

by hand and by wheel, and was fired to a much harder consistency. Vessel shapes were much more diverse, ranging from simple plates to exotic bowls, jars, cups, and boxes, often slipped with a lustrous black finish or decorated with a wide array of incised and painted designs. Many of the ornately decorated larger vessels appear to be forerunners of the bronze vessels of later times. Another major accomplishment of Lung-shan artisans was the development of metallurgy, which for the most part led to the production of simple copper artifacts, such as vessels, small trinkets, and tools. The Yellow River Valley held rich deposits of copper and tin, which would prove to be critical building blocks of the early urban economy. Towards the end of the period, metalwork-

ers began alloying copper and tin to produce bronze implements, as evidenced by a few rare finds at several sites, including a bell, a bronze knife, and a fragment of a bronze vessel.

The origins of Chinese writing also can be traced to this period. However, unlike in Mesopotamia and the Indus, the first inscriptions did not serve accounting purposes, but rather arose from ideographs (a pictorial symbol denoting an object) used in rituals. The origins of these ideographs lay in shamanistic divination ceremonies, when hot metal was applied to the shoulder-blade bones—or scapulas—of oxen, water buffalo and other large mammals (and sometimes tortoise shells) to produce patterns of cracks. The meaning of the cracks was then interpreted by priests. The widespread use of scapulas gave rise to the term scapulimancy, or "shoulder-blade divination". Eventually, the cracks and fissures in the bones took on regular meanings—many were pictographic in nature—and an ideographic script evolved. The divination rituals involved communication with the royal ancestors, who acted as intermediaries to a supreme being known as Shang Di;

thus the earliest texts dealt almost exclusively with religious matters. Later texts included information on historical events and a variety of aspects of ancient Chinese life. During the Lung-shan period, the divination rituals served to enhance the status of community leaders, and later became an important part of the life of the urban royal court in Shang dynasty times.

Unfortunately, our knowledge of the size and extent of Lung-shan communities is somewhat limited, though it is evident that many would easily be considered sizeable towns by modern standards. However, a large number of residential structures have been excavated. These were built of wattle and daub or brick in a variety of shapes, ranging from simple circular huts to rectangular structures with two or more rooms. Some structures were built on low platforms, and plastered floors and walls were quite common. Burials are often found underneath or next to houses. Other community features included storage pits, wells, pottery kilns, and cemeteries.

The large cemeteries found at many sites indicate that Lung-shan society was becoming increasingly stratified. At the site of T'ao-ssu, the cemetery contains several thousand burials, a thousand of which have been excavated. The finest of these displayed substantial wealth: the individuals were laid in wooden coffins and covered with cinnabar powder, and often wore fancy headdresses and jewelry. The burial furnishings, in some cases numbering up to 200 items, included large numbers of decorated pottery vessels, pig

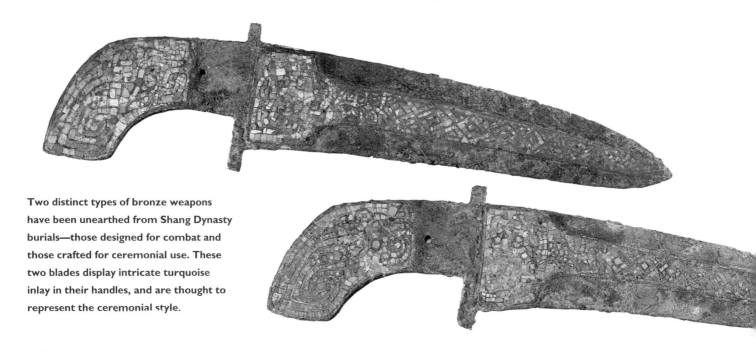

Two distinct types of bronze weapons have been unearthed from Shang Dynasty burials—those designed for combat and those crafted for ceremonial use. These two blades display intricate turquoise inlay in their handles, and are thought to represent the ceremonial style.

skeletons, a variety of painted wooden objects, jade artifacts, combs, hair-pins, and musical instruments. The latter included drums made from pot-tery and from crocodile skin, and an object known as a music stone. In later times, these musical paraphernalia are associated with royalty. The more elegantly furnished, larger, and deeper graves were invariably those of males. These were often accompanied by the shallower graves of females, which had fewer quantities of goods. The other end of the social scale was charac-terized by simple burials with few or no furnishings.

Although we know little about Lung-shan political structure, the large forti-fied towns with ranked societies suggest a fairly high degree of organization. There is also widespread evidence of warfare, as indicated by the presence of weapons in burials and of the signs of massacres, with bodies then dropped into wells. Prisoners were sacrificed and decapitated, and their skulls may have been used as drinking cups. While the reasons behind this violence are not known, it would appear that a privileged warrior class was emerging, and that the elites of many communities were increasingly concerned with defense while at the same time conducting raids on their neighbors. This, admittedly, is speculative, but it is not difficult to imagine the Yellow River Valley as a mosaic of chiefdoms competing for political power and resources on a regional level.

Towards the end of this period, around 2100 B.C., a considerably advanced com-munity emerged at Erh-li-t'ou, in the central Henan region. According to later

This delicately carved jade ornament, dating to about 2000 B.C., just prior to the Shang Dynasty, was made before the advent of metal tools. Its function, however, remains unknown. Measuring only 3.2 inches (8.2 centimeters) in diam-eter, it is too small to be a bracelet, but may have been an earring.

Simple circular huts made of wattle and daub, sometimes built on a low platform, were a common feature of Lung-shan towns. With the emergence of the community of Erh-li-t'ou, urban development in China entered a new and more complex phase. Among the buildings excavated at the site, located in central Henan Province, were two palatial structures. The floor plan of one of these is shown at right.

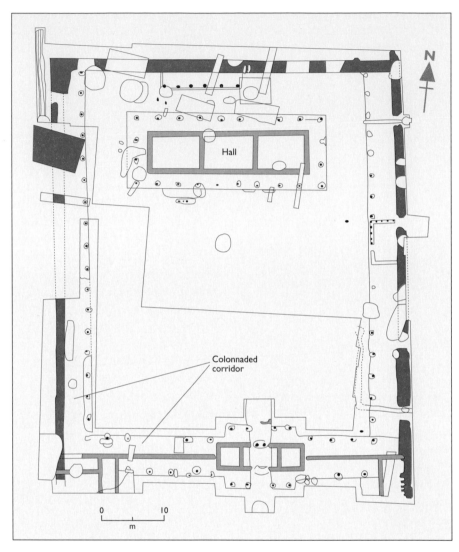

Hall

Colonnaded
corridor

0   10
    m

accounts, which are largely legendary, this region was the home of the oldest known Chinese dynasty, known as the Xia (or Hsia). Erh-li-t'ou may have been a capital of the Xia people. The site, discovered by Chinese archaeologists in 1957, covers an area of almost 1.5 square miles (4 square kilometers), and includes the foundations of two large structures that may have been public structures or palaces, as well as numerous houses, storage pits, pottery kilns, wells, the remains of a bronze foundry, and roads paved with gravel or compacted earth. As a detailed map and most of the reports of the excavations at the site have yet to be published, we can only discuss some of the highlights of the site, as summarized by Chang.

The largest palace, which measured 328 by 354 feet (100 by 108 meters), had a large courtyard surrounded by a colonnaded corridor. On its north

Shang Dynasty ceremonial bronzes were among the finest bronze pieces produced in the ancient world. Elegant tripod vessels known as *ding*, such as the example shown here, held offerings to the gods and spirits. The vessels varied in size from tiny to enormous, and usually bore decorations of zoomorphic designs.

side were the remains of a large hall, built of timber, with wattle-and-daub walls and a gabled roof. The second palace, which was smaller, had a similar layout, but the hall included three rooms and was surrounded by a veranda. A drainage system, made of pottery pipes, has been found beneath the courtyard. Both palaces had numerous burials, including the remains of at least one very elaborate tomb. Many of the surrounding dwellings were quite elaborate. Rectangular in shape, they contained several rooms, and were often accompanied by well-furnished burials with lacquered coffins and other goods. In a few instances, the burials of the palaces and houses display evidence of a violent end, suggesting ritual sacrifices associated with the construction of the structures.

Excavations at Erh-li-t'ou have unearthed large quantities of material goods, including pottery and implements made from stone, jade, shell, and bone, as well as bronze artifacts. The latter include ritual drinking cups, a plaque inlaid with turquoise, musical instruments, and weapons, such as arrowheads, halberds and knives. What is clear from the remains and artifacts at Ehr-li-t'ou is that a new elite had emerged, one that had the power and wealth to rule over large areas. This elite was also beginning to take on the trappings of royalty, indicating that Chinese civilization had arrived at the threshold of statehood.

Several dozen sites of the Ehr-li-t'ou culture have been reported in Henan Province, suggesting that the region may have been politically unified. This is also suggested by legendary accounts of Xia kings, who reportedly had a succession of capitals. The last king, known as Chieh, had a capital at Chen-Hsün, a yet-to-be identified site in northwestern Henan. According to historical accounts, he was defeated by a warrior-king known as T'ang, who founded the Shang Dynasty.

THE SHANG DYNASTY

With the emergence of the Shang state (1766 B.C. to 1100 B.C.), China entered the historic period. The ideographic script had become widespread by this time, and historic texts appear not only on oracle bones, but on bronze vessels and other objects as well. From later sources, we know that Shang court archivists also kept detailed records on bamboo, wood, and silk, but these have not survived. The existing texts are almost solely concerned with ritual and political matters, and include information on court activities and the history of Shang rulers.

From these early inscriptions, we know that the Shang Dynasty had 30 rulers, the earliest of whom, T'ang, established his first capital at a place called

Exquisite workmanship was a hallmark of Shang Dynasty craft production. Jade ornaments, such as this dragon pendant, were decorated with the comma, or *huai*, pattern which was popular between the sixth and third centuries B.C.

This halberd blade probably served as a ceremonial weapon during the late Shang Dynasty. Crafted from jade, the blade measures 10 inches (26.6 centimeters) in length, and would have been hafted to a pole through the hole near its base.

Po, which was located at an undetermined location in eastern Henan. He also set up other capital cities in Henan, and these are also referred to in the texts as Po. Subsequent rulers moved the capital six times, to Xiao (or Ao), Xiang, Keng, Pi, Yen, and Yin-hsü.

Under the Shang, civilization in northern China came into full flower. True cities appeared, with monumental public architecture, royal households, and royal cemeteries. The society was ruled by a supreme king, whose position was reinforced by privileged classes of priests and warriors, and by large standing armies with horse-drawn chariots (horses had been domesticated in Lung-shan times). Craft specialization spawned legions of artisans, whose exquisite workmanship in bronze and jade reflected a highly distinctive and unified art style throughout the realm. The ideology of the state was a convenient marriage of ritual and politics, and court activities included the age-old practices of divination, the maintenance of a ritual calendar, and human and animal sacrifices.

Archaeologists have located and excavated one of the earliest capitals, Ao, which lies under the modern city of Zhengzhou (Cheng-chou) near the Yellow River in northern Henan. Because of its location under the modern city, we do not have an accurate estimate of the size of the ancient capital, but it was evidently quite extensive, covering more than 5 square miles (12 square kilometers). Limited excavations in the downtown area have exposed a vast precinct that housed the royal compound. This covered an area of 2 square miles (5.2 square kilometers), and was enclosed by an earthen wall 33 feet (10 meters) high. The wall, one of the earliest great public works in Chinese history, was approximately 4 miles (6.4 kilometers) long. This royal compound contained the royal palaces, temples, and residences of the nobility, of which only partial foundations have been exposed. Beyond the compound are the remains of many other structures, including residential quarters, cemeteries, and craft workshops. The latter included at least two bronze foundries, bone workshops, and a village of potters with their kilns. One of the foundries, which lies to the north of the royal compound, included several large houses that may have belonged to bronze metalworkers. These were rectangular in shape, and contained two rooms laid out on an east-west axis and an altar set against one of the walls. The walls were likely made of wattle and daub, and the structures were covered by gabled thatched roofs; the floors and altars were plastered. In and around the houses were the remains of many clay molds for bronze weapons and vessels, fragments of crucibles, and cores for the legs of bronze vessels. To judge from the furnishings of their burials, which included elegant ritual bronze vessels, these craftsmen enjoyed high social status, and may have been members of the upper class.

The other foundry, which lay to the south of the royal compound, covered an area of approximately 2.5 acres (1 hectare), and included many remains of crucibles and clay molds for making a variety of weapons and ritual vessels.

Residential areas have been identified on all four sides of the compound, and their houses and burials reflect a broad range of wealth and social stratification.

The last and greatest of the Shang capitals was at Yin-hsü, which was located 95 miles (152 kilometers) north of Ao, near the modern city of Anyang. The site was discovered in 1928, and has been the subject of excavations ever since. The city consisted of a network of royal compounds, villages, and cemeteries, and covered approximately 9 square miles (24 square kilometers). The core of the city lies near the modern hamlet of Xiao-tun, 1.5 miles (2.4 kilometers) northwest of Anyang. Excavations have unearthed the remains of the main royal compound, which included the foundations of at least 53 large structures and a large number of enormous burials, spread over an area of 2.5 acres (1 hectare). The layout of the structures was carefully planned, and archaeologists have identified a residential section, with large rectangular royal houses, a temple sector, and a public ceremonial area. The royal residences and temples were built on rectangular or square platforms, with foundations of compacted earth that sometimes reached a depth of 10 feet (3 meters). Next to many of the foundations were burials of animals and humans, which are believed to have been the remains of ritual sacrifices associated with the construction of the buildings. The structures were built with a timber frame, the posts of which were anchored to stone or bronze pillar bases, with wattle-and-daub walls, and gabled thatched roofs. These were often quite large; the longest measured 48 by 279 feet (14.5 by 85 meters), the largest 131 by 230 feet (40 by 70 meters). The long rectangular buildings often had two or more rooms, or rooms alternating with open porch areas. In addition to the royal residences and temples, there were many smaller structures at Xiao-tun. These were semisubterranean pithouses, and served as residences for staff and servants, storage structures, and workshops. Some of the storage structures served as granaries, while others contained pottery, bronze weapons, musical instruments, and oracle bones. One structure held more then 300 turtle plastrons (the ventral plate of the turtle shell) and 10,000 oracle bones, and is believed to have been a royal archive. The workshops included bronze foundries and shops for the working of stone, jade, bone, and shell. Thousands of artifacts made from these materials have been recovered from storage pits next to the workshops.

Many of the settlements that made up the ancient capital of Yin-hsü also contained palaces and temples, residential houses of varying sizes, workshops, and cemeteries. The most spectacular Shang Dynasty remains are the huge tombs that have been uncovered at Xiao-tun and at several of the cemeteries surrounding Yin-hsü. These are monumental constructions, consisting of large, oblong pits with ramps leading down into them. One of the most massive tombs, known as No. 1001, measures 46 by 62 feet (14 by 19 meters), and is 33 feet (10 meters) deep. Ramps lead into it from the north, south, east, and west; the southern, and longest, ramp is approximately 100 feet (30 meters) long. Inside the pit, a wooden chamber contained the coffins of the main individual and his retinue. Around the

Measuring 8 inches (21.2 centimeters) across and 5.5 inches (13.9 centimeters) in height, this bronze urn, or *kuei*, probably served as a cooking or drinking vessel. It dates to the middle to late An-Yang phase of the Shang Dynasty (12th to 11th centuries B.C.).

pit and in the ramps were numerous sacrificial human burials, often decapitated. The tomb was richly furnished with a large number of artifacts, including some of the finest Shang bronze, pottery, and jade. What is most striking about these tombs is the wealth that accompanies many of the individuals. One tomb, believed to be that of a royal consort, contained 1600 artifacts and 7000 cowrie shells brought from the coast. The objects included more than 560 bone artifacts, 590 jades, and 440 bronzes of the highest quality. Shang ceremonial bronzes were among the finest of the ancient world. Most were large urn-like vessels, with large hollow legs or stands, handles, and covers, elaborately decorated with relief masks, incised motifs, and ideographic texts. Others were made to represent animals. Large stone sculptures, often depicting animals, also accompanied many graves. Another striking feature of several of the tombs are the remains of horses and chariots, which were often accompanied by bronze fittings, leather armor, shields, and caches of weapons. These are, no doubt, a reflection of the importance of warfare in Shang society. The number of human sacrificial burials that accompanied some of the finer tombs is astounding; in one tomb, the ramps were layered with 59 headless skeletons and 73 skulls. These tombs were clearly the graves of the most elevated members of the Shang court—the kings, their consorts, and nobles—and the departure of these members of the elite was marked by awe-inspiring ceremonies and rituals.

During the Shang Dynasty and in the Zhou period that followed, the dead typically were buried in pit-tombs similar to the one shown at right. The body of the deceased was placed in a deep, rectangular pit called a *shu-hsüeh*, the walls of which were vertical or sloped slightly inward or outward. Sometimes a smaller inner pit was dug in which the coffin, or *kuan*, was placed. This left a ledge, or *erh-t'seng-t'ai*, around the coffin, on which offerings were placed. The floor and walls of the tomb were often plastered, the walls sometimes painted as well. Larger graves had one, two, or four ramps sloping into the pit. The bodies of sacrificed humans and animals were sometimes also buried at various places in the tomb, or else in the ground around it.

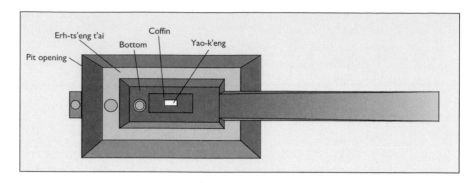

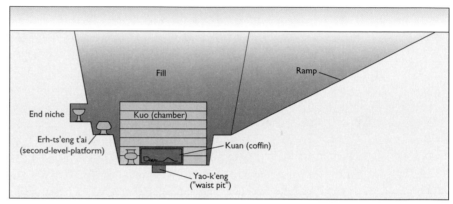

As noted, Shang society was ruled by dynastic kings who traced their lineage to divine ancestors. The power of these rulers, and that of their noble retinue, was based on a network of blood kinship lines that formed the framework of the structure of the state. Below this group was a large court following made up of lesser nobles, warriors, and bureaucrats, who managed the day-to-day life of the realm. Other prominent members of the society included powerful traders and master craftsmen. Below them was the bulk of the population—farmers and herders, craftspeople, boatmen, and servants and slaves. Beyond the capital, provincial lords held sway in fortified towns that were in turn surrounded by smaller villages and hamlets. The backbone of the state was the army, which could marshal 10,000 men on short notice. State activities and the wealth of the elite were financed through a complex tribute system, in which provincial lords supplied the capital with everything from grain to the finest products of their craftsmen, as well as exotic trade goods from farther afield, such as shells from the coastal regions. It was this combination of military might and tribute that led scholars to refer to early Chinese societies as "tributary states".

At the peak of the Shang state, the kings ruled over a large territory that covered most of the northern and central regions of Henan Province and the southern and western areas of Shandong Province. Their constant wars of conquest often extended their domain beyond this area to include portions of neighboring provinces as well, but their control over these areas was often only temporary.

Towards the end of the 12th century B.C., the Shang were conquered by their western neighbors, the Zhou (or Chou), whose power had been growing in the final century of the Shang era. The Zhou adopted and incorporated most of the infrastructure of the Shang state. They added their own contributions, among which were the invention of iron metallurgy, the plow, and large-scale irrigation systems. However, the Zhou were unable to create a fully unified political domain. Their state was made up of many semi-independent provinces, ruled by warlords who were in constant conflict with one another. This state of affairs lasted until 221 B.C., when the Zhou were conquered by Xuang Ti, the great ruler of the Ch'in Dynasty, who unified all of China into a single empire. Despite these changes, the great advances made by the Shang survived, and continued to mold Chinese culture and society for many centuries.

THE RISE OF THE SHANG CITIES

Most of the ingredients that gave rise to the Chinese state appeared during the period known to archaeologists as the Lung-shan Horizon. Population was increasing, an agricultural way of life was well established, and the introduction of rice and irrigation diversified the crop base and, together with the grain crops, assured the potential for surplus. Other critical resources, such as copper, tin, jade, and shell, were readily available, and provided the impetus for growing craft specialization, trade, and the inevitable social differentiation that accompanied the accumulation of wealth. Regional trade brought many communities into close contact with one another, permitting the spread of many shared cultural features, such as ceramics, bronze-working, and architecture, that characterize early Chinese civilization. Increased social complexity is evident in the fortified towns that appeared across the landscape, and the emergence of regional political power bases is indirectly attested to by the evidence for widespread warfare.

Warfare was a key ingredient in the rise of political complexity, and played a major role in the consolidation and maintenance of the Shang cities and their economy. Coupled with this was the central role of shamanism—as reflected in the tradition of ceremonial divination rituals—that came to forge an important link between ideology and politics, and ultimately legitimized the role of an emerging power elite.

Kwang-chih Chang has proposed that the above factors, working from the village level upward, created a sphere of economic and political interaction that laid the foundations for the Shang state. While we lack information on the specific political events that led to the creation of the first Xia Dynasty, the prevailing conditions clearly provided an optimal setting for the rise of centralized authority and the crystallization of the Shang urban tradition.

Just a few miles northeast of Mexico City is the ruined metropolis that the Aztecs called Teotihuacán, or "City of the Gods". Looking south restored Pyramid of the Sun rises impressively above the altars, shrines, and temples that line the wide, central avenue known as the Street of

MESOAMERICA: CITIES OF THE GODS

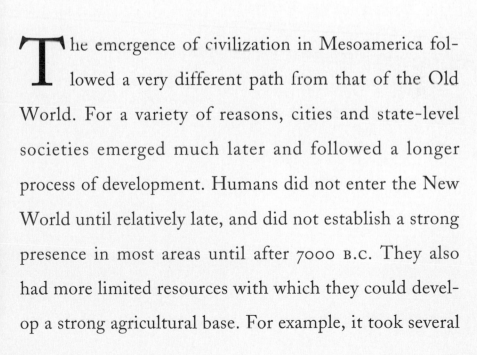

from the Pyramid of the Moon, the partially
the Dead.

The emergence of civilization in Mesoamerica followed a very different path from that of the Old
World. For a variety of reasons, cities and state-level
societies emerged much later and followed a longer
process of development. Humans did not enter the New
World until relatively late, and did not establish a strong
presence in most areas until after 7000 B.C. They also
had more limited resources with which they could develop a strong agricultural base. For example, it took several

thousand years to develop high-yield strands of corn from a simple, grass-like plant called *teosinte*, and the only truly domesticated animal was the dog. In contrast, the first settlers of the Near East enjoyed access to huge stands of wild wheat and herds of wild goat and sheep that could be readily domesticated. As a result, it took longer for large concentrations of human population to build up in most areas of Mesoamerica.

The first Mesoamerican cities did not appear until the final centuries of the first millennium B.C., and differed markedly from their counterparts in the Old World. In the first place, they were not built around wheeled transport. We know from surviving toy carts that the people of Mesoamerica were familiar with the wheel, but the lack of beasts of burden and the mountainous terrain did not encourage the development of wheeled vehicles. As a result, Mesoamerican cities were focused around large plazas, where the people could attend ritual ceremonies and buy and sell goods in large open markets. The elite sectors of these cities, on the other hand, tended to have more restricted access to ensure privacy.

Another difference between Mesoamerica and the earliest Old World states was the absence of metallurgy, which did not appear in Mesoamerica until long after the first cities emerged. Without metal or beasts of burden—and thus chariots—warfare was limited to armies of foot soldiers bearing stone weapons. With such armies, Mesoamerican city-states could only secure relatively small political domains, much smaller than those of their Old World counterparts.

Mesoamerica, which encompasses central and southern Mexico, all of Guatemala, Belize, and El Salvador, and western Honduras, can be divided into two major ecological zones, namely highland mountain country and tropical lowlands. The mountains are part of the Cordilleran system that runs down the North and South American continents from Alaska to Patagonia. In northern Mexico, this system splits into two parallel mountain chains, known as the eastern and western Sierra Madre ranges. They rejoin in central Mexico, and continue south into Oaxaca as the southern Sierra Madre. Beyond the low-lying area at the Isthmus of Tehuantepec, the mountains arise again and continue through Chiapas, Guatemala, El Salvador, and on down Central America. Along this mountain chain are several large basins, such as the valleys of Mexico, Puebla, and Oaxaca, where pockets of rich soil provided ideal conditions for agricultural development, population growth, and the rise of complex social systems. The temperate highlands have a moderate climate, with both rainy and dry seasons; the larger valleys lie between 5000 and 7500 feet (1500 and 2300 meters) above sea level, and are watered by year-round rivers and perennial streams. The Valley of Mexico, the largest of all, also has several large salt- and fresh-water lakes that provided the early inhabitants with fish and salt.

The tropical lowlands encompass the large coastal plains that surround the Gulf of Mexico, and include the low-lying peninsula of Yucatán and the Petén jungle of northern Guatemala. Several large rivers flow into the Gulf,

Mesoamerica encompasses the highland mountain country of central and southern Mexico, and the tropical lowlands of Guatemala, Belize, Honduras, and El Salvador. A number of fertile basins interspersed along the Sierra Madre mountain chains provided ideal conditions for the emergence of complex, state-level societies.

creating rich alluvial bottomlands in Veracruz, Tabasco, and southern Campeche. Several other rivers flow from the Guatemalan Petén into the Caribbean Sea. Most of the lowlands—now mostly given over to agriculture and cattle ranching—were once covered with lush tropical forests. The climate is hot, and characterized by dry and wet seasons.

EARLY SETTLEMENTS

The oldest known permanent settlement in Mesoamerica is found at a site known as Zohapilco on the shores of Lake Chalco in the southern Valley of Mexico. Its earliest occupation dates to approximately 6000 B.C., the beginning of the Archaic and Early Formative periods (6000 B.C. to 1200 B.C.), when local hunter-gatherers settled down to exploit an abundant variety of resources available in the lake and surrounding areas. They hunted, fished, and collected shellfish, supplementing these activities with the harvesting of teosinte grasses, amaranth, and other wild plant foods. Little is known of their settlement, as the excavations conducted by Christine Niederberger, an archaeologist with the National Institute of Anthropology and History of Mexico, have revealed only the presence of hearths, plant and animal remains, and chipped and ground stone tools, the last used for processing plant foods. The finds at Zohapilco are highly unusual, as they document a sedentary lifestyle long before the advent of agriculture. Peoples living in other highland areas at this time were still leading a nomadic hunter-gatherer way of life, scheduling their movements to the seasonal availability of animal and plant foods in different ecological zones. At Zohapilco, the year-round availability of lacustrine resources—such as fish, aquatic birds, turtles, and amphibians—allowed early settlers to establish fully sedentary communities while they experimented with plant foods that would eventually become their main agricultural staples.

The long process of plant domestication that led to the emergence of farming communities elsewhere in Mesoamerica has been extensively documented by American archaeologists Richard MacNeish and Kent Flannery and their colleagues in the valleys of Tehuacán and Oaxaca. In both of these regions, excavations have unearthed evidence of a gradual process of domestication of the main plant foods—corn, beans, squash, chilis, fruits, and other foodstuffs—that eventually made up the staples of the Mesoamerican diet. This process culminated in the appearance of sedentary villages around 2500 B.C. in the highlands, and shortly after 2000 B.C. in coastal regions of the Pacific and the Gulf of Mexico. These villages consisted mostly of clusters of wattle-and-daub houses covered with palm-thatch roofs. Their inhabitants used a variety of stone tools for hunting, and grinding stones for processing plant foods. They also began making simple ceramic vessels for household purposes, as well as baked-clay human and animal figurines, which may have had ritual functions.

THE OLMEC AND THEIR NEIGHBORS

Sometime around 1200 B.C., at the beginning of what is called the Middle Formative period (circa 1200 B.C. to 400 B.C.), the first complex culture emerged in the coastal lowlands of southern Veracruz and western Tabasco. Known as the Olmec, they are often referred to as the *Cultura Madre* (Mother Culture) of Mesoamerica, and are best known for the colossal stone heads they sculpted of their rulers. The Olmec were not recognized by archaeologists as a distinct culture until the 1920s, and the first investigation of an Olmec site did not take place until National Geographic Society archaeologist Matthew Stirling began excavations at La Venta in 1938. The excavations lasted eight years, and uncovered a large complex of earthen mounds surrounding a plaza. Beneath this plaza was an amazing array of artifacts, including caches of polished jade celts (implements), figurines, and jewelry, a tomb made of basalt columns, a basalt sarcophagus, and an immense serpentine mosaic pavement. These discoveries were all the more impressive in light of the fact that all the basalt, jade, and serpentine had to be imported from elsewhere.

At first it was thought that the Olmec culture belonged in the Classic Period (A.D. 300 to 900), because such a level of complexity was not believed to have been possible in earlier time periods. However, Miguel

The colossal carved basalt heads found at La Venta, on the Gulf Coast of Mexico, are testament to Olmec skill both in artistry and logistics The transportation of the stones—weighing up to 40 tons—from quarries more than 60 miles (100 kilometers) away required a well-organized labor force.

One of the most interesting discoveries made at La Venta was that of a group of human figurines with oversized heads. All the figures except one were carved from greenstone, and were positioned around a single figure made of granite. The group is thought to have been buried as an offering.

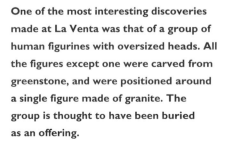

Covarrubias, a distinguished Mexican writer and artist, proposed that the style of Olmec art and sculpture suggested a much earlier, Preclassic date (hence his designation of the Olmec as the Cultura Madre); Stirling also supported this early dating. The two were eventually vindicated when a second set of excavations at La Venta, conducted during the 1950s by U.C.L.A. archaeologists Robert Heizer and Philip Drucker, came up with radiocarbon (C14) dates that pointed to an occupation between 900 B.C. and 400 B.C.! Subsequent excavations at the site of San Lorenzo by Michael Coe of Yale University during the 1960s revealed that Olmec culture arose even earlier, around 1200 B.C.

This seated figure is incorporated into a carved stone block at La Venta known as Altar 4, which may have been a throne for newly appointed Olmec rulers. The figure is thought to represent an ancestral hero emerging from the primordial earth-cave in which life began.

The early rise of Olmec culture was made possible in part by the rich environment of the southern Gulf Coast region. Several rivers flow through the area, creating deep deposits of rich alluvial soils. Farming on the river levees and nearby productive lands can yield up to two crops a year. In addition, there was a variety of wildlife for hunting, and fish and shellfish abounded in the rivers and along the nearby coasts.

The Olmec had four major settlements—San Lorenzo, La Venta, Laguna de los Cerros, and Tres Zapotes—plus dozens of smaller communities. The core of La Venta is a large, rectangular plaza flanked by low, terraced mounds and walls. Dominating the south side of the plaza is a large earthen mound, whose base measures 230 by 400 feet (70 by 120 meters); it reaches a height of 100 feet (32 meters). Aside from the finds mentioned above, the site had a large number of huge basalt sculptures, including several thrones, stelae, and colossal heads of rulers, some of which weigh up to 40 tons. The sculptures are perhaps the most telling evidence of a complex social organization among the Olmec. The basalt had to be transported, mostly by water, from sources over 60 miles (100 kilometers) away, which posed tremendous logistical problems. These activities clearly reflect the existence of a powerful elite who could muster a substantial labor force, which would have also included skilled boatmen to oversee the construction of large rafts and navigate them from the source to the site. Once at the site, the sculpting would have been supervised by master craftsmen, who worked closely with the rulers and their priests in designing the multiple religious themes—and elite portraits—displayed in the art.

Powerful carvings adorned the walls of monuments in several Oaxaca Valley towns. Originally termed *danzantes* (dancers), these figures were later thought to represent prisoners captured in battle. This carving is from San José Mogote, and its accompanying glyph, "One Earthquake", is the oldest known inscription in Mesoamerica.

In addition to their famous monumental sculpture, the Olmec left behind a varied repertoire of smaller artwork, including exquisite works of jade and a sophisticated ceramic tradition that featured slipped and painted vessels and figurines. They were also busy traders, importing massive amounts of raw materials for their sculptures and artwork, some of which was later exported all over Mesoamerica.

Archaeologists have yet to determine the extent of the major Olmec sites, and we have no idea as to the nature of their political structure or the territories of individual sites. Excavations have revealed house-mound clusters at both La Venta and San Lorenzo, suggesting that they were town-sized communities with several thousand inhabitants. But they were clearly not cities. This fact, and the absence of any evidence of a state bureaucracy, a standing army, or political boundaries, has led most scholars to suggest that they were a chiefdom-level culture—a ranked society ruled by chiefs—one step below that of a state. Alternatively, Phillip Drucker has suggested that they may have been an incipient "primitive state."

During the Olmec florescence along the southern Gulf Coast, communities throughout the highlands also began to grow and to develop higher levels of complexity and social organization. Large towns with populations of 1000 or more people appeared at several locations in the valleys of Mexico and Oaxaca, and in several smaller valleys as well. Their inhabitants made a variety of stone tools, elegant painted pottery and clay figurines, items of basketry, and ornamental artifacts of shell and jade. Large sectors of the population were involved in part-time craft specialization, and often worked with materials supplied through far-reaching trade networks. Among these materials were obsidian, a volcanic glass which came from various sources in the highlands; jade (probably from Guatemala, perhaps supplied through Olmec traders); and shell from coastal regions. The people lived in wattle-and-daub houses with thatched roofs, often set around a core of public buildings constructed on top of large stone masonry platforms around open plazas. While most of these public buildings were dedicated to ritual purposes, others housed members of the elite. Evidence of growing social stratification is also reflected in many burials, which contained fancy pottery and artifacts made from imported raw materials.

The impressive Zapotec metropolis of Monte Albán was built on a mountaintop in the Valley of Oaxaca. Monte Albán is centered around the huge plaza shown above. The plaza is lined with civic and religious buildings and palaces built on pyramidal platforms. Scattered over the surrounding hills are the remains of several thousand residences, as well as canals and reservoirs.

In several regions, there is evidence of growing cultural and sociopolitical complexity, with major towns controlling large numbers of surrounding rural villages and hamlets. Chalcatzingo, in the modern state of Morelos, is believed to have been a major trading center, with a population estimated at between 1400 and 3600 people between 700 and 500 B.C. The community was located around a central plaza surrounded by terraced mounds and numerous large stone monuments, which may depict local rulers and historical themes. At San José Mogote, another large town in the Valley of Oaxaca, a stone monument depicts an important captive with an accompanying day-sign glyph, "One-Earthquake"; in the nearby foundations are the remains of several human sacrificial victims. This glyph is the oldest known hieroglyphic inscription in Mesoamerica, and attests to the existence of a 260-day calendar at that time (circa 700 B.C. to 500 B.C.). In later times, rulers were often named after their birthdate, suggesting that the

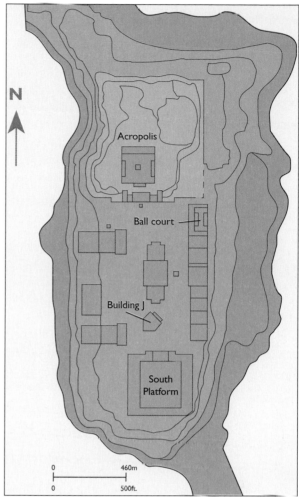

The main plaza at Monte Albán, shown in the map above right, is oriented north-south. The Acropolis dominates the north end, with a ball court situated nearby. Carved reliefs in two temples in the plaza have glyphs recording Zapotec conquests and tributary towns. The arrowhead-shaped Building J contains 50 "conquest slabs" that record subjugated towns. Imagery on stelae on the sides of the South Platform suggest the existence of trading ties between Monte Albán and its northern neighbor, Teotihuacán.

individual depicted on the above monument may have been a defeated ruler; alternatively, the day-sign glyph may record the date on which he was sacrificed.

As the Middle Formative period drew to a close, Mesoamerica was made up of a mosaic of chiefdoms that displayed many of the accouterments of an advanced culture: densely inhabited towns, craft specialization, class stratification, large public buildings and evidence of public rituals (including human sacrifice), monumental art, the beginnings of calendrics (calendar systems) and writing, and the emergence of a ruling class. The Olmec were the most advanced of these societies, but they entered a period of decline around 500 B.C., and were eclipsed by the rise of more powerful political units in the highlands. One of the largest of these crystallized in the valley of Oaxaca, where the growing city of Monte Albán emerged as the primary political center.

The first true urban culture to appear in Mesoamerica was that of the Zapotecs (500 B.C. to A.D. 700), who established their capital, Monte Albán, on a mountaintop in the middle of the Valley of Oaxaca. Archaeological research in the Valley of Oaxaca has been going on for over a century. Much of the early work at Monte Albán and other sites in the valley was conducted by a group of scholars whose accomplishments made them legendary figures in the history of Mexican archaeology: Leopoldo Batres, Alfonso Caso, Ignacio Bernal, and Jorge Acosta. Research in recent years has also seen the participation of American scholars, including Richard Blanton, Gary Feinman, Kent Flannery, Stephen Kowalewski, Joyce Marcus, John Paddock, Ronald Spores, and Marcus Winter, among many others.

Around 500 B.C., the valley of Oaxaca was occupied by several chiefdoms, possibly one in each of the three arms of the valley. For reasons that are not entirely clear, a new town was established on top of Monte Albán, a 1300-foot-high (400-meter-high) mountain that lies at the juncture of the three arms of the valley. It has been suggested that the new town was founded as the capital of a confederation of the chiefdoms that had previously ruled the different parts of the valley—much as Washington, in a central location between the northern and southern states, was established as the capital of the United States. An alternative theory is that the rulers of San José Mogote, the largest town in the valley in earlier periods, decided to move their seat of power to a preeminent position in the center of the valley.

The capital grew rapidly, and by 200 B.C. had surpassed the neighboring towns in the valley. In fact, it seems that the elite of San José Mogote and other towns had moved to the new mountaintop capital. By this time, the population is estimated to have reached between 10,000 to 20,000 people, and Monte Albán had become a fully developed urban center. It included several monumental buildings, a 1.8-mile-long (3-kilometer-long) defensive wall, a reservoir, several hundred carved monuments, and several residential sectors. Few of the original buildings of this early period survive, as they have been covered over by later construction. One of the earliest and most impressive is the building known as Mound L, which contained a gallery of panels with 300 carved figures, known as the *danzantes*. These are nude male figures with drooping limbs and half-closed eyes, some displaying blood from castration and penis mutilation. Many are accompanied by glyphs, which may record their names; some also have a "rattle" glyph that is believed to represent death. It is now widely believed that these were war captives, rulers of subjugated towns who were ritually sacrificed after their defeat in battle. Thus they were displayed by the rulers of Monte Albán as trophies of their military conquests. This display of military might and the huge defensive wall that surrounds part of the site are strong indications that warfare played a prominent role in the rise of the Zapotec state.

A series of 300 carved stone *danzantes*, including the one shown below, surrounds one of the earliest buildings at Monte Albán. The custom of creating carved monuments to represent captives, first begun at San José Mogote, was prevalent at Monte Albán.

By A.D. 700, shortly before it went into decline, Monte Albán had a population of 25,000 to 30,000 people. The city core covered 2.5 square miles (6.5 square kilometers), and dispersed residential areas spread onto adjoining hills, covering a total area of 7.7 square miles (20 square kilometers).

By this time, the city was an impressive metropolis. At the center lay a huge rectangular plaza, oriented north-south, flanked by scores of civic and religious buildings and elite palaces built on large pyramidal platforms. At the north end of the plaza a massive elevated acropolis still stands, featuring a complex of courtyards, temples, and residences that probably housed the rulers of the city. East of this acropolis, in the northeast corner of the plaza, is a large ball court, where the ritual Mesoamerican ball game was played. The east and west sides of the plaza are lined with large palatial buildings that also included altars and shrines and likely served as temples and residences of the nobility and priests. In and around the acropolis and plaza buildings, archaeologists have uncovered some of the richest tombs ever found in Mesoamerica. The individuals in them were interred with beautiful ceramics, shells, pearls, and ornate jade masks, earspools, and necklaces.

In the center of the plaza is a group of four temples. One of these, known as Building J, was built in the shape of an arrowhead. Like most of the other structures around the plaza, it dates from the period known as

A tiger or jaguar god was prominently depicted in Zapotec sculpture, although little is known of its exact role in religious life. Shown here is a ceramic representation of the deity.

The large ball court at Monte Albán is situated in the northeast corner of the plaza, east of the Acropolis. Ball courts are a prominent feature of most Mesoamerican sites. Although the rules of play are unclear, the courts themselves are thought to have represented the symbolic boundaries between the real and the supernatural.

Monte Albán II (200 B.C. to A.D. 100). Its abnormal shape and orientation have led some scholars to suggest that it may have been an astronomical observatory, a notion for which there is little or no compelling evidence. In his excavations of the building in the 1930s, Alfonso Caso uncovered several internal galleries with more than 50 stone relief panels, most of which contained symbols for places and their accompanying glyph names, as well as upside-down human heads. Caso proposed that these were a record of places that had been subjugated by Monte Albán, and that the heads were those of defeated rulers. As Zapotec writing remains largely undeciphered, many of these glyphs cannot be read. However, Joyce Marcus of the University of Michigan has tentatively identified four of the place-names, which lie between 50 and 93 miles (between 80 and 150 kilometers) of the capital, and suggests that the "conquest slabs" represent a record of the Zapotec domain and its tributary towns. In some respects this is a continuation of the earlier danzante tradition, although the written medium elevates them to the status of formal state documents.

The largest structure at the site is the South Platform, a massive pyramid built sometime after A.D. 300; it was recently excavated by Marcus Winter. On the sides of this building were several stelae displaying individuals whose clothing and regalia suggest that they were emissaries from the great capital of Teotihuacán in the Valley of Mexico. As we shall see below, there is strong evidence of close ties between these two cities.

Beyond the Main Plaza, on the mountaintop and on terraces on the slopes of the mountain, are the remains of several thousand residences. For the most part, these are groups of mounds that supported wattle-and-daub structures. Archaeologists have identified 14 distinct neighborhoods, each with its own small plaza and civic-ceremonial structures. Some of the larger mounds in these neighborhoods may have been residences for the lesser elites. Heavy concentrations of ceramic and stone artifacts at specific locations in several of these neighborhoods may be the remains of workshops. Interspersed between the neighborhoods are the remnants of canals and reservoirs, which likely provided the city with drinking water and irrigation for small garden crops.

At its height, Monte Albán controlled a large territory beyond the valley, although the full extent of its domain has not yet been determined. On the basis of the archaeological record and the place-name glyphs mentioned previously, there is evidence to suggest that its northern frontier may have reached Cuicatlán Cañada, a river canyon some 50 miles (80 kilometers) away; its southern frontier may have reached the Pacific Coast, near Tututepec, 90 miles (145 kilometers) away. While we do not know much about the nature of Zapotec political organization, analogies with later Mesoamerican cultures suggest that the state was ruled by a powerful elite who held military control over the conquered areas, and who in turn supplied the capital with a variety of tribute goods, including foodstuffs, ceramics, textiles, basketry items, shells and pearls from the coast, and exotic materials for making jewelry. The accumulated wealth of the capital allowed the Zapotec elite to project their power far beyond their domain, and engage in trading and diplomatic activities with other Mesoamerican states, such as Teotihuacán in central Mexico.

Toward A.D. 700, Monte Albán went into a period of severe decline, and was eventually abandoned; the exact causes of its demise are not yet known. Stephen Kowalewski of the University of Georgia has suggested that a major factor may have been the overpopulation of the valley, which led to land and food shortages, and the eventual disintegration of the political systems that held the Zapotec state together. Interestingly, the collapse of

The Pyramid of the Sun, some 210 feet (61 meters) tall, dominates the lesser temples along the Street of the Dead in Teotihuacán. Built over a natural cave, the pyramid was considered sacred—a ritual gateway to the Underworld, which, according to the creation myth, was the birthplace of the human race.

Monte Albán occurred shortly after the fall of Teotihuacán, hinting that the destinies of the two capitals may have been linked.

TEOTIHUACÁN (300 B.C. TO A.D 700)

The Aztecs called it the City of the Gods, and still carried out ritual activities in the ruins of the long-abandoned city when the Spanish conquistadors arrived in the 16th century. By that time, eight centuries had passed since Teotihuacán had been destroyed in a massive conflagration, but the memory of its past glory lived on.

Archaeological research at Teotihuacán dates back to the 19th century and has continued almost without a break to this day. Among the earliest investigators were Leopoldo Batres and Manuel Gamio, who conducted the first large-scale excavations at the site. Gamio's stratigraphic work, which began in 1917, led to the unveiling of the chronological sequence of cultures that had inhabited the region—from Preclassic villages to Classic Teotihuacán to the Postclassic Toltec and Aztec states. In its broad form,

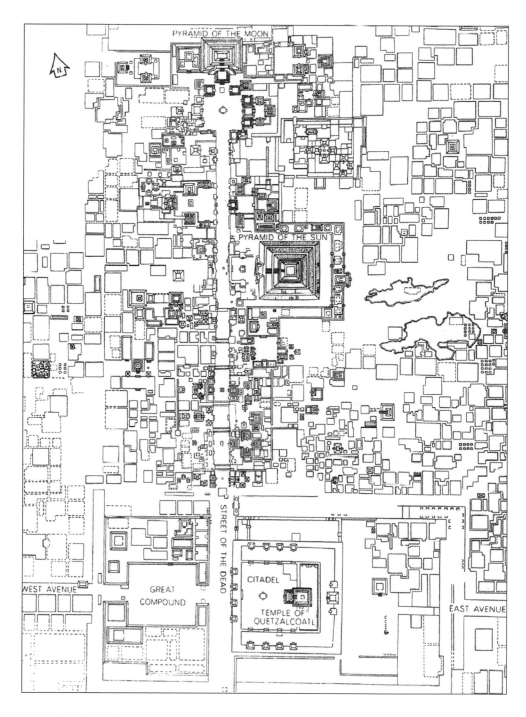

Central Teotihuacán was divided into quadrangles along its main north-south axis, the Street of the Dead, which was lined with palaces and temples. East-west avenues further subdivided the city into neighborhoods. Even the San Juan River was canalized to conform to this regular layout.

The Temple of Quetzalcoatl (or, the "Feathered Serpent") at the south end of Teotihuacán's Street of the Dead, is decorated with superb three-dimensional and bas-relief sculptures. Huge carved serpent heads with feathered collars alternate with geometric carvings of another deity. Undulating serpent bodies in bas-relief connect the images.

this chronology stands to this day. Hundreds of other scholars have since worked at Teotihuacán. Among the most prominent initiatives have been the Teotihuacán Project, a massive excavation program initiated by the Mexican Government in 1960, directed by Ignacio Bernal and Jorge Acosta and their successors. Scores of Mexican scholars have carried on these excavations, the most recent being Rubén Cabrera, Linda Manzanilla, and Eduardo Matos Moctezuma. From the 1960s onward, several North American projects, working in tandem with the Mexicans, have also contributed to our knowledge of the ancient city. These include William Sanders' Basin of Mexico Survey Project, which conducted detailed settlement-pattern surveys of the entire valley; the Teotihuacán Mapping Project, directed by René Millon with the assistance of Bruce Drewitt and George Cowgill; and a survey and inventory of the mural paintings at the site, conducted by Arthur Miller.

The city of Teotihuacán lies in the valley of the same name, in the northeastern sector of the Valley of Mexico, just a few miles beyond the eastern

outskirts of Mexico City. It lies in the center of the valley, next to the San Juan River, which empties into Lake Texcoco, now almost completely drained. The valley was a rich agricultural area, and its inhabitants maximized its potential through the construction of irrigation canals, dams, and terraces. The lake also provided a steady supply of fish, waterfowl, and salt, as well as access to canoe networks which brought in food supplies and trade goods from all over the Valley of Mexico.

As noted above, the Valley of Mexico has a long history of occupation, dating back to Archaic times (circa 5000 B.C.). The first towns began to appear after 1000 B.C. Several of these communities had large public buildings, evidence of occupational specialization, (indicated by the remains of pottery and obsidian workshops), as well as cemeteries with richly endowed burials that reflect the emergence of social stratification. Sometime after 300 B.C., two major urban centers had emerged, one at Teotihuacán in the north, and the other at Cuicuilco in the south. The latter town, built around a massive, stepped, circular pyramid, is estimated to have had a population of 20,000 people concentrated in an area of almost 1000 acres (400 hectares). Sometime during the first century B.C., a series of eruptions from the nearby Ixtli volcano buried Cuicuilco and its agricultural fields, leaving Teotihuacán as the sole major center in the valley.

The origins of Teotihuacán lie with a cluster of communities located next to a series of caves and tunnels that became major shrines in the final centuries before the Christian era. These settlements were built around plazas with three temples, and were designed as ritual gateways to the Underworld, which was the home of many of the gods, and, according to Mesoamerican creation myths, the birthplace of the human race. Thus, Teotihuacán was founded in a very sacred location, and its role as a religious shrine contributed overwhelmingly to its power and prestige for several centuries to come. Another factor that played a major role in the rise of Teotihuacán was the availability of several sources of obsidian in neighboring valleys to the north. As the city grew in size and importance, the number of obsidian workshops proliferated, and Teotihuacán became a major supplier to other communities in the Valley of Mexico and beyond.

The image of a human face on this ceramic brazier lid unearthed at Teotihuacán is richly adorned with earspools and a feather headdress. Much of the ornamentation, especially the central plume, seems to evoke Quetzalpapalotl, the butterfly god.

By A.D. 150, Teotihuacán had grown into a full-scale urban metropolis covering an area of 8 square miles (20 square kilometers), and its population had swelled to an estimated 50,000 to 80,000 inhabitants. The population density of the city continued to grow for several centuries more, until it reached its peak in the seventh century, with estimates ranging between 125,000 and 200,000 people. At that time it was probably one of the largest cities in the world.

During the first two centuries of the Christian era, the rulers of Teotihuacán embarked on an ambitious program of public works that dwarfed anything previously seen in Mesoamerica. Rivers and springs were channeled, and irrigation systems extended to encompass large parts of the valley, thereby ensuring a plentiful supply of foodstuffs. The city was well planned, and was laid out in a grid of quadrangles along a north-south axis defined by a central boulevard known as the "Street of the Dead". Other major avenues run parallel to the Street of the Dead, and are in turn intersected by several east-west avenues, which lead to lesser streets reaching throughout the city. Even the San Juan River, which flows through the city, was channeled to conform to the grid.

Most of the great monuments that visitors see today were erected at this time. Among the most imposing are the pyramids of the Sun and the Moon. The former, the largest structure in the Valley of Mexico, lies almost halfway down the east side of the Street of the Dead. Erected above an ancient cave shrine, the great pyramid rises from a base that measures approximately 700 feet (213 meters) to a side, and attains a height of 210 feet (61 meters). At the top stood a temple, or possibly twin temples, which are now gone. By one estimate, it would have taken 10,000 workers 20 years to build the pyramid! The second-largest structure of the city is the somewhat smaller Pyramid of the Moon, which lies at the north end of the Street of the Dead, facing a large plaza. The other structures around this plaza include several temples and at least one elite residence, known as the Palace of Quetzalpapalotl (Quetzal-Butterfly). This is a large masonry structure with several courtyards surrounded by rooms, and is famous for its sculpted and painted relief panels. Excavations of several other sumptuous palaces near the center of the city have uncovered many brightly painted murals and sculpted relief panels.

The city has hundreds of temples, dedicated to a wide pantheon of deities. Recent excavations have revealed that the dedication of many of these was accompanied by rituals involving human sacrifice. One of the hallmarks of Teotihuacán religious architecture is a decorative feature known as the *talud-tablero* design. This consists of a vertical sunken panel (a *tablero*) set over a sloping apron (the *talud*), and is found on the facades of the tiers of hundreds of pyramids at the city. Many of the temples and palaces along the Street of the Dead display this feature.

Halfway down the Street of the Dead, on opposite sides of the street, are two huge compounds arranged around large plazas. The western one, known as the Great Compound, may have been the main marketplace of the city. To the east lies the Citadel, a huge courtyard flanked by 13 pyramids. The dominant structure is the Temple of Quetzalcoatl, named after the many sculpted heads of the Feathered Serpent that decorate its tiered facades. Quetzalcoatl was an ancient Mesoamerican wind deity; he was also a patron god of rulers, priests, and merchants. Alternating with the Feathered Serpent heads are the carved masks of another deity, believed to be that of the War Serpent. Flanking the Temple of Quetzalcoatl are the remains of two enormous palaces, which may have been the residences of the rulers of the city. The combined imagery of the temple is an imposing display of the basic ingredients that formed the power base of the Teotihuacán state: water (the source of sustenance of its agricultural base), religion, trade, militarism, and divinely ordained rulership.

Beyond the temples and palaces at the center of the city are more than 2000 walled residential units known as apartment compounds. These are multifamily dwellings, often set around a central courtyard containing a shrine. The residences of the wealthy were made of stone with timber roofs, while the homes of commoners were built of adobe. The dead were buried underneath the houses and courtyards, and the goods that accompanied them reflect marked differences in social status. The variation in residential units, coupled with the burial goods, mirrors the social makeup of the city. The palaces housed the elite, which included the rulers and their extended families, priests, top military officials, major merchants, and senior bureaucrats. A second social tier, represented by the fancier apartment compounds, is likely to have included engineers, master craftsmen, artists, merchants and traders, and lesser officials. The bulk of the population, which lived in the lesser compounds, was made up of craftsmen, farmers, and laborers.

Craft specialization was an industrial concern at Teotihuacán, and the basis for its wealth. Archaeologists have uncovered the remains of hundreds of workshops throughout the city. The vast majority of these were obsidian workshops, though many also produced pottery; clay figurines; lapidary work in jade, serpentine, and shell; and stone tools made of flaked chert and ground basalt. There were also undoubtedly workshops dedicated to the production of perishable articles that have not been preserved, such as cotton cloth and clothing, basketry, cordage, leather, wooden goods, and featherwork. It is estimated that, at its height, the city employed 30,000 craftsmen and artisans, or between 15 and 25 percent of its population. Many of their goods, particularly obsidian tools and cores (from which tools could be made), were traded all over Mesoamerica. A unique green obsidian, whose only source was the mines of Pachuca in the nearby modern state of Hidalgo, has been recovered from sites as far away as the Maya lowlands of Yucatán and Guatemala.

While Teotihuacáno merchants plied the trade routes of Mesoamerica, large numbers of traders and pilgrims from distant lands also journeyed to the metropolis, bringing with them a wide array of goods and cultural influences. Foreign pottery and artistic motifs from the Gulf Coast, Oaxaca, and the Maya area abound. One neighborhood, known as the Merchants' Barrio, has unusually high concentrations of Totonac pottery from the Gulf Coast of Veracruz, as well as ceramics from the Maya lowlands. Traders from Oaxaca had their own barrio, complete with Monte Albán-style tombs and funerary urns.

Seen as a whole, the city of Teotihuacán was a cosmopolitan center unlike any other in the world at the time, and its trade and influence reached all corners of Mesoamerica. The great scope of this influence is evident not only in the spread of its trade goods, but also in the wide distribution of the talud-tablero motif so characteristic of its architecture. Temples with talud-tableros, and variations on this theme, are found throughout Mesoamerica, at Monte Albán, in Oaxaca, and at cities in the lowlands and highlands of the Maya area. That Teotihuacán was an industrial craft center, a major trading metropolis, and a religious mecca for pilgrims and travelers, there is little doubt. But what was the nature of its political apparatus? Oddly enough, we know next to nothing about this aspect of the city, owing in part to the lack of a written script with historical information. While the murals and relief panels contain a large corpus of notational glyphs, which appear to be pictographic and ideographic in nature, little progress has been made towards their decipherment. Part of the problem is that scholars cannot agree on which language was actually spoken at Teotihuacán. Even so, these glyphs are primitive in nature, and suggest that Teotihuacán was at the threshold of developing a written script. This is somewhat surprising, since both the neighboring Oaxacans and the Maya both possessed systems of writing at that time.

Without this kind of information, there is little we can say about the political structure of the city, or of the extent of its territorial domain. There is little question that this was a highly complex state-level society, and that its political domain included the Valley of Mexico and several adjoining areas. The nature of Teotihuacán's influence beyond this area is nebulous. While its commercial and cultural influence spread throughout Mesoamerica, there is scant evidence of outright military conquest or of political control beyond the central highlands.

Sometime around A.D. 700, Teotihuacán was destroyed. In the words of René Millon, the end was "fiery and cataclysmic." Large parts of the city were put to the torch, and most of the buildings along the Street of the Dead were laid waste. The process of destruction appears to have been chillingly systematic and ritualistic, and focused primarily on temples, palaces, and other public buildings. Great fires were set in front and on top

Multifamily dwellings arranged around a courtyard were the most common type of housing at Teotihuacán. More than 2000 of these apartment compounds, a typical example of which is shown here, were built. The homes of the wealthy were built of stone, with adobe used for lower-status residences.

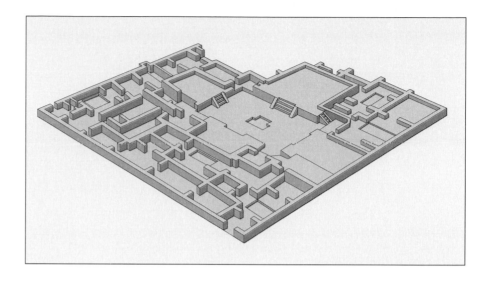

of pyramids, and temples and palaces were literally torn apart and burnt; hundreds of statues were smashed, and their fragments scattered. Excavations in the royal palaces of the Citadel have uncovered the remains of richly adorned individuals, whose dismembered skeletons suggest they met a violent end. There is also considerable evidence of looting, which probably followed shortly after the conflagration. Many apartment compounds were also burnt, and most were abandoned within a relatively short time. Small squatter populations continued to occupy several neighborhoods for many years thereafter, but the city's role as a commercial, religious, and political center came to an end.

The systematic dismantling of the religious and political core of the capital was clearly intended to ensure that Teotihuacán would never again rise to a position of power in Mesoamerica. But who did it? And why? We have no idea. In fact, we do not even know if the destruction of the city was wrought by outsiders, or by an outraged local populace. The abrupt demise of Teotihuacán remains one of the most perplexing questions in Mesoamerican archaeology, and a major objective of future research.

Following the fall of both Teotihuacán and Monte Albán, the Mexican highlands embarked on a protracted period of competition and warfare between small city-states that was to last for several centuries. For a brief period, between A.D. 900 and 1200, the Toltec capital of Tula emerged as the preeminent military and commercial center in the northern Valley of Mexico, but it never was able to achieve the power and glory of the older cities. Such a scale of grandeur would not be rekindled until the early 15th century, with the rise of the Aztec capital of Tenochtitlán, whose short-lived empire dominated most of Mesoamerica for a brief century before the arrival of the Spaniards in 1519.

With its grand, frontal stairway, numerous courts, and tower rising from a vast stone platform, the complex known as the Palace, at the Late Chiapas, could have been the residence of a Maya ruler. During the 19th century, the first reports of ancient cities such as Palenque began to

7

THE ROYAL CITIES OF THE MAYA

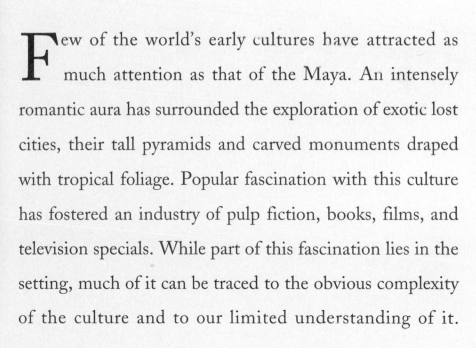

Few of the world's early cultures have attracted as much attention as that of the Maya. An intensely romantic aura has surrounded the exploration of exotic lost cities, their tall pyramids and carved monuments draped with tropical foliage. Popular fascination with this culture has fostered an industry of pulp fiction, books, films, and television specials. While part of this fascination lies in the setting, much of it can be traced to the obvious complexity of the culture and to our limited understanding of it.

Classic site of Palenque in the Mexican state of unlock the mysteries of Maya civilization.

Much of the attraction lies in the apparent contradictions in the development of the Maya. They represent the most highly developed culture in the New World up to that time, yet they lacked beasts of burden, wheeled transport, important mineral resources, and metallurgy. They built sophisticated cities and large public works in a tropical environment that was hostile and lacking in resources. With the unique exception of the much later kingdoms of Southeast Asia (such as Angkor Wat), no other ancient tropical culture in the world reached such a high pinnacle of achievement.

The emergence of complex societies in the Maya lowlands was for many years seen as the result of influence from the highland regions of Mesoamerica. Although the highland cities emerged and blossomed at an earlier stage, recent research indicates that the Maya urban tradition has an autonomous pattern of development going back several centuries before the Christian era. In the last two decades, archaeologists have identified several large settlements that show a surprising degree of complexity as early as Late Preclassic times (400 B.C. to A.D. 300).

The existence of a complex urban society in the tropics of Mesoamerica was almost unknown to the world until the middle of the 19th century, when John Lloyd Stephens published the two-volume *Incidents of Travel in Central America, Chiapas, and Yucatan* (1841). Profusely illustrated with the excellent engravings of his companion traveler, the English architect Frederick Catherwood, this widely published work announced to a surprised public the existence of the remains of a complex civilization buried deep in the forests of southern Mexico and northern Central America. A second set of volumes, this one on the ancient monuments of northern Yucatán, followed in 1843. Many of the major ruins uncovered by Stephens and Catherwood—Copán, Palenque, Chichén Itzá, and Uxmal—are now tourist meccas, and their initial explorations also opened the way for many other explorers and archaeologists. Among these are the legendary pioneer explorers of the late 19th century, including Désiré Charnay, Teobert Maler, Alfred Maudslay, and Edward Thompson, whose efforts led to the detailed documentation of the architectural remains and carved monuments of scores of ancient Maya cities. Their work has been continued in the 20th century by large teams of professional scholars working for research institutions who have conducted extensive regional surveys of the Maya area, and initiated excavations at several key sites. Among these institutions are Harvard University, the Carnegie Institution of Washington, the Middle American Research Institute of Tulane University, the National Institute of Anthropology and History of Mexico, the University of Pennsylvania, the New World Archaeological Foundation of Brigham Young University, and several others. The number of scholars involved in Maya research has mushroomed from a small handful at the turn of the century to several hundred today, and annual conferences on advances in Maya research are held in

The arch at Labna, in Yucatán, was one of many beautiful illustrations by the English architect Frederick Catherwood, who accompanied John Lloyd Stephens in his travels through the Maya area from 1839 to 1842. The publication of their travel accounts introduced the world to the previously little explored realm of Maya civilization.

diverse locations, from Central America to Canada and Europe. Research on the Maya has become an international effort, and involves scholars from Mexico, Guatemala, Belize, Honduras, El Salvador, the United States, Canada, England, France, Spain, Germany, and Japan. Current field projects include the excavations at Copán, Honduras, where several institutions are working under the aegis of the Honduran government; this is currently the largest archaeological project in the hemisphere.

The Maya lowlands—the main focus of this chapter—encompass the entire Yucatán Peninsula and adjoining areas of eastern Tabasco, northern Chiapas, the Guatemalan Petén, Belize, and northwestern Honduras. While most of this area lies below 600 feet (180 meters), the territory rises to the Puuc hill country of central Yucatán, the Maya Mountains of Belize and the southeastern Petén, and the foothills of the Maya highlands that run from Chiapas to Honduras. The flat plains of northern Yucatán are devoid of rivers, but the underlying water table is easily accessible through the thousands of *cenotes* that dot the landscape. These natural sinkholes formed when open cavities in the limestone collapsed, exposing the water table. Farther south, several rivers—the Grijalva, Usumacinta, and the Candelaria—flow into the Gulf of Mexico. On the eastern side of the peninsula, the Hondo, New, Sarstún, and Motagua rivers all pour into the Caribbean. Most of the Maya lowlands are covered by tropical vegetation. The area enjoys a hot climate most of the year, with a long rainy season from May to November, followed by cool winter storms in December and January and a hot dry season from February to May. Many areas of the southern lowlands have rich soils for agriculture, and a great variety of tropical crops are grown.

EARLY VILLAGES

Very little is known about the earliest settlements of the Maya lowlands during the Early and Middle Preclassic (or Formative) periods (1300 B.C. to 400 B.C.). The perishable remains of their houses and other materials have not survived well in the humid, acidic soils of the tropics. Moreover, many Maya communities were built up in the same location over a period of many centuries, so that the remains of many early communities are buried deep underneath later constructions. There are scattered reports of Archaic period remains, and we know from pollen cores that maize was being cultivated by 2000 B.C. However, the oldest known remains of permanent settlements date to after 1300 B.C., and are found in deep deposits at Copán, in Honduras, and at Cuello, in northern Belize. At these sites, excavations have uncovered the foundations of small domestic structures, with hearths, simple utilitarian ceramics, artifacts made from ground stone and flint, and the bones of large, edible mammals. At Copán, several obsidian artifacts were found that probably were traded from the nearby highlands of Guatemala. Agriculture is well documented at Cuello, where the remains of maize, beans, squash, and chili peppers have been recovered. The presence of decorated slipped pottery at Cuello hints at the existence of an earlier ceramic tradition. This inference would suggest that earlier settlements are still to be found.

Following the onset of the Middle Formative period, around 900 B.C., villages in the Maya lowlands began to grow in size and complexity. At Cuello, Norman Hammond of Boston University and his colleagues have uncovered a courtyard surrounded by raised platforms, elaborate slipped ceramics, and a wide range of artifacts, including jewelry made from the shells of the nearby Caribbean as well as objects made from obsidian and jade, both of which were traded from the Guatemalan highlands. A cemetery at Copán dating to this period, excavated by William Fash, included a

The civilization of the Maya emerged in the forested lowlands that cover much of southern Mexico and northern Central America. The lowlands are traditionally divided into two sections: the flat northern half is dominated by the low-lying Yucatán Peninsula. In the southern section, which lies mainly in Guatemala, the terrain is more rolling, with steep limestone ridges running northwest to southeast.

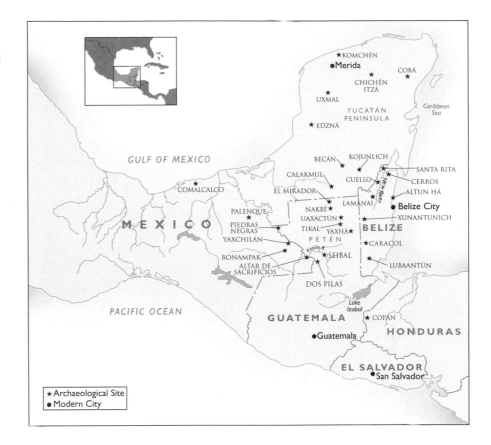

large number of individuals buried with jade beads, greenstone celts, and pottery decorated with Olmec motifs that were derived from the ceramics of the early chiefdoms of the Gulf Coast of southern Veracruz and Tabasco. Remains of Middle Preclassic communities have also been reported from several other sites in the Maya lowlands, including Colhá and Santa Rita in northern Belize; Nakbé, El Mirador, Seibal, and Altar de Sacrificios in the Guatemalan Petén; several sites in eastern Tabasco; and Komchén in northern Yucatán. Olmec ceramic designs and artifacts have been reported from several of these sites, suggesting sustained contacts with the southern Gulf Coast region.

The presence of sophisticated ceramics, long-distance trade goods, and burials with high-status items at several Middle Formative sites is a strong indication that Maya society was beginning to exhibit signs of craft specialization and social differentiation. On the other hand, the absence of public constructions suggested that most communities were still simple villages, without any of the outward displays of major social complexity. This view has recently been challenged by new discoveries at Nakbé, in the northern Petén. In excavations that began in 1989, archaeologist Richard Hansen uncovered what may be the oldest known public architecture in the Maya lowlands. Beginning around 600 B.C., the inhabitants of this community built two clusters of large stone platforms and pyramidal structures. These include a pyramid 150 feet (46 meters) in height and a massive platform, 100 feet (30 meters) high, with three mounds on top, known as a triadic pyramid. Detailed reports on the excavations at Nakbé are not yet available, but the initial finds clearly suggest that the beginnings of large-scale social complexity were present in the Maya area much earlier than was originally thought.

EARLY TOWNS AND THE FIRST CITIES

Around the beginning of the Late Preclassic period (400 B.C. to A.D. 250), several villages in the Maya lowlands began to grow into substantial communities. One such village was at Komchén, in northern Yucatán, which was excavated by E. Wyllys Andrews of Tulane University and his colleagues in 1980. Here several large stone masonry platforms were erected around a rectangular plaza. These platforms reached heights of 10 to 16 feet (3 to 5 meters) and often had smaller platforms on top, which in turn supported perishable structures made with wattle-and-daub walls and thatched roofs, probably close to 25 feet (7.5 meters) in height. From this plaza a *sacbé*, or elevated causeway, runs 820 feet (250 meters) to the northeast to another large platform with a pyramidal mound on top. The sacbé is the oldest of its kind in the Maya area. Surrounding these public buildings are approximately 1000 house platforms, which decrease in size as one moves to the periphery of the site. It is conservatively estimated that the town had at least 3000 inhabitants.

At Nakbé, around 300 B.C., one of the pyramidal structures was enlarged and remodeled, and six large stucco masks were molded onto its facade. These masks, which are found at several later sites, are the earliest of their kind in the Maya area, and attest to the origins of a pattern of monumental public ritual displays. Further reinforcing this notion was the discovery of a limestone stela with a depiction of two individuals dressed in regal accouterments. Richard Hansen believes that these are historic personages (and possibly rulers) who are reenacting a Maya origin myth. Later stelae of the Classic period almost invariably portray rulers and members of the elite. At Nakbé, other indicators of increasing differences in social status include decorated bichrome pottery; exotic trade goods, such as marine shells and obsidian; and burials of individuals whose teeth contained jade inlays. Taken together, the finds at Nakbé point to the existence, by 200 B.C., of a ranked society with an emergent ruling class, a formal religious system, and a complex economy.

After 200 B.C., Komchén and Nakbé fade out of the picture, to be replaced by much larger towns, some of which reached urban proportions. One of the largest was El Mirador, located 8 miles (13 kilometers) to the

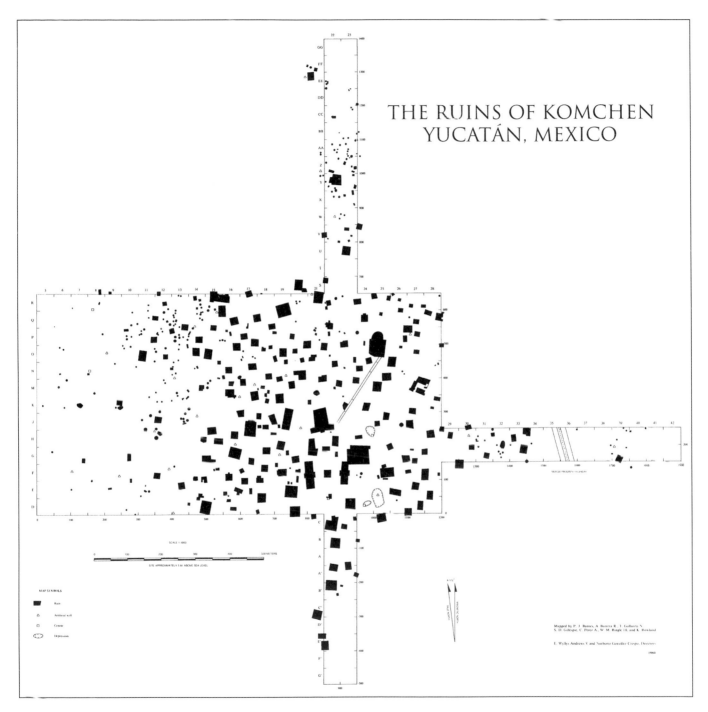

THE RUINS OF KOMCHEN
YUCATÁN, MEXICO

At Komchén, in Yucatán, archaeologists have mapped a mass of mounds, house platforms, and larger structures that give an idea of the density of settlement at this early Maya city. At the center is a group of large stone masonry platforms grouped around a plaza. A *sacbé*, or raised causeway, runs northeast to link this plaza with another large platform topped by a pyramidal mound.

The huge size of El Mirador, a Late Preclassic city located in a remote part of northern Guatemala, became clear during excavations that began in the late 1970s. The map at right shows only a small portion of the site. In the center is the **West Group**, the heart of El Mirador. From the center of the city, causeways radiated out to satellite communities. A number of causeways are visible on the left of the map.

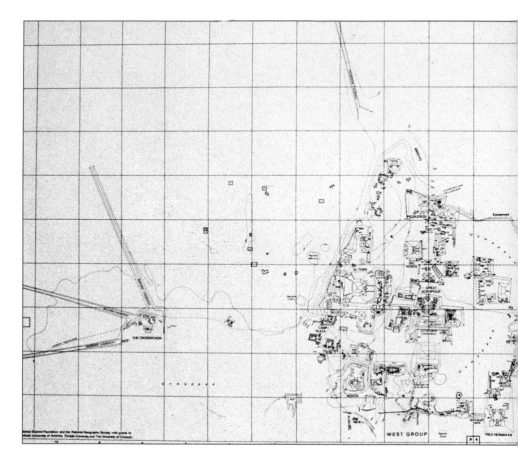

northwest of Nakbé. Originally reported in 1926, this site was surveyed and excavated between 1978 and 1982 by a team of archaeologists under the direction of Ray Matheny, of Brigham Young University, and Bruce Dahlin, of Howard University. Covering an area of approximately 10 square miles (16 square kilometers), the site includes the remains of several huge architectural complexes and a network of low walls and sacbés. The core of the site lies in the West Group, and contains five complexes, each of which houses temples, terraces, courts, and elite residences. The largest of these complexes, known as El Tigre, covers an area of 153 acres (62 hectares), and includes a 180-foot-high (55-meter-high) pyramid with three temples on top; this triadic temple arrangement, seen earlier at Nakbé, is also found at several other complexes at the site. Flanking the staircase of one of the temples in the El Tigre Complex are the remains of two large stucco masks of deities with human and jaguar features. Of particular interest are the large, clawed jaguar paws that extend out from each head; these and other related features appear in later Classic art as emblems of royalty. Some 2600 feet (800 meters) to the east of the West Group lies the Danta Complex, the

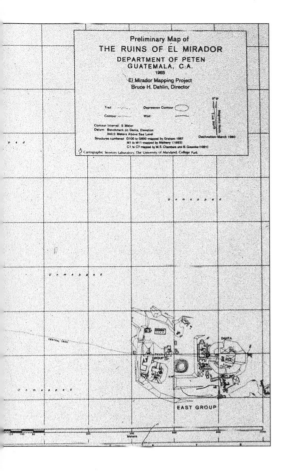

other main precinct at the site. Built on a leveled-off hill, this complex covers an area of 37 acres (15 hectares), and includes a series of terraces and courtyards surrounded by temples and palaces. It is dominated by the Danta pyramid, which rises to a total height of 230 feet (70 meters) above the jungle floor at the base of the hill. The Danta Complex is one of the largest constructions ever built by the ancient Maya.

Given the sheer size and remote location of the site, the work at El Mirador was limited, and barely provided a glimpse into the complexity of the city. The full extent of the site is not known, nor do we have even an approximate idea of the size of its population, although it must have numbered in the thousands or perhaps tens of thousands. We know little about its economy, other than the obvious fact that it depended heavily on agriculture. Excavations have uncovered large amounts of finely made pottery and two possible lithic—or stone—workshops, as well as shells brought from the Caribbean and obsidian traded from the highlands of Guatemala, all indications of an advanced level of craft specialization and trade. Needless to say, we know next to nothing about its history or politics. The explorations did reveal the existence of stelae and altars, though only one of these was carved; it depicts an individual, and bears traces of a glyphic text that contains primitive versions of later Maya glyphs. A glyph was also found incised on a potsherd, but scholars have yet to determine whether these texts constitute an effective system of writing. What is most puzzling about El Mirador (and Nakbé as well) is its location, far from any rivers, lakes, or major resources. What prompted its inhabitants to settle there? Was it a crossroads for trade? Or did it merely develop in a rich agricultural area? Many more years of work at the site will be necessary before we can begin to answer these questions.

The excavations at the Guatemalan site of Uaxactún, during the 1920s, led to a completely new understanding of the Classic Maya. However, the discovery of a Late Preclassic structure that became known as Pyramid E-VII-sub—so-called because it was found buried beneath much later constructions—pushed the beginning of Maya ceremonial construction back much further than archaeologists had previously thought. The pyramid, which is visible through the trees in this photograph, is best known for the large panel masks that line its central stairway.

Several other sites also grew into large communities in the waning years of the last millennium B.C. Among these was Tikal, 65 miles (105 kilometers) southeast of El Mirador, which is better known for its Classic Period remains. As at El Mirador, though on a smaller scale, the rulers of Tikal built more than 100 large public buildings in two areas now known as the North Acropolis and the Mundo Perdido (Lost World) Group. In the former complex, archaeologists have unearthed some of the most elaborate tombs and burials of the Formative period in the Maya area, including painted murals, beautiful ceramics, jade and shell artifacts, and stingray spines (used in elite bloodletting ceremonies). There is little question that a powerful elite had emerged at the site; in fact, by the second century A.D., a royal lineage was in place. By the third century, writing was fully developed, and hieroglyphic inscriptions refer to rulers by name.

Hundreds of Late Formative settlements have been reported throughout the Maya area, although most of these were only small villages. Nonetheless, it is evident that the population was growing fast, and that many people were already living in sizeable communities. The larger sites that flourished in the later half of the Late Formative period include Uaxactún, just north of Tikal; Edzná, Becán and Calakmul in the Mexican state of Campeche; and Cerros and Lamanai in northern Belize. As the Formative levels of these sites lie under the remains of later periods, our knowledge of them is fragmentary. One exception is Cerros, a largely intact Late Formative trading port on the north coast of Belize, excavated by David Freidel and his students from Southern Methodist University. Here, a large shoreline acropolis dominated the town, which controlled the growing trade networks between the Caribbean and the inland cities of northern Belize and the Petén. At Cerros and the other sites, large groups of monumental buildings were erected, and there is ample evidence of craft specialization and trade, social differentiation, and an elite ruling class. The architecture, ceramics, and religious iconography are remarkably similar at all these sites. Trade appears to have been an important factor in the development of a common cultural base across the region. Obsidian and jade were traded from the highlands to communities throughout the lowlands, and salt from the north coast of Yucatán flowed into the southern cities. Large-scale coastal trading brought many distant communities into close contact, and Maya canoes reached many of the offshore islands, such as Cozumel and the Belizean cays.

The growing trade networks served as a medium for the spread of religious ideas throughout the region, as attested to by the religious paraphernalia, stelae, and stucco masks. These display a remarkably homogeneous body of signs and symbols, and embody the rituals and beliefs of a formal religious system. Monuments also now bore hieroglyphic dates that were based on a "long-count" that originated in 3114 B.C., a date that must have

With giant stucco masks on its stairway, the partially excavated temple at Cerros, Belize, stands guard over the ruined Caribbean coastal town. This shoreline city was a trading center whose mercantile network extended from the coast to the inland cities of northern Belize and the Guatemalan Petén.

had special mythical significance to the Maya but is now lost to us. These monuments also carried hieroglyphic texts written in a fully developed system of phonetic writing that recorded prominent events in the lives of their rulers. Two such monuments, from the adjoining highlands and Pacific Coast of Guatemala, have long-count dates of A.D. 36; another, a monument from the southern lowlands known as the Hauberg Stela, records a date of A.D. 199, accompanied by a depiction of a ruler with a bloodletting scene, a prominent ritual performed by the elites of the later Classic period.

By the end of the period, around A.D. 250, the Maya had developed most of the features of a complex society. Many communities had thousands of inhabitants, and there is considerable evidence of full-scale craft specialization and long-distance exchange, as well as the use of calendar and writing systems. The society was highly stratified, and its ruling class had become closely identified with its religious rituals and world view.

At this point, the inevitable question arises: was this a full-fledged urban, state-level society? Most scholars would probably reply in the affirmative, though perhaps with some qualifications. Others would answer "no" on the grounds that there is no evidence for a multitiered settlement hierarchy of cities, towns, and villages that is indicative of complex political systems. This feature cannot be identified until A.D. 500, and then only in some areas. Unfortunately, detailed settlement data is lacking for most Late Formative communities, so we do not know the full extent of the settlements or how many inhabitants they had, or the size of their political domains. Nor do we know if they had bureaucracies and standing armies—the evidence for warfare in the Formative period is almost nonexistent.

Moreover, the origins of writing in the Maya lowlands are still not well documented; the earliest readable texts date to the second century B.C., and the oldest recorded long-count date is 199 B.C. Still, monuments in the nearby highlands suggest that the origins of Maya writing go back even further. At present, our records of royal lineages only go back to the beginning of the second century A.D. Were earlier rulers true kings, or merely powerful chiefs? Much hinges on this question, as we know very little about the political structure of the Maya communities of the Formative period. Still, the sheer size of sites like El Mirador and Tikal clearly suggests the existence of a complex society with a powerful ruling class that could direct the construction of massive public works and the operation of an increasingly complex economy. Yet, as we shall see in the next chapter, large monumental enclaves were also built in the Andes long before the appearance of fully developed urban states. It appears that the Maya communities of the Late Formative period had reached urban, or near-urban proportions, and that they likely controlled the surrounding countryside. By most standards they would be considered primitive city-states, but whether they were something more complex remains a question for future research.

CLASSIC MAYA CULTURE (A.D. 250 TO 900)

Beginning around A.D. 250, fully developed urban communities flourished throughout the Maya area, from northern Yucatán to northwestern Honduras and from eastern Tabasco to Belize. The earliest cities appeared in the southern lowlands. They include the well-known cities of Tikal, Uaxactún, Yaxhá, Piedras Negras, Altar de Sacrificios, Seibal, and Dos Pilas in the Guatemalan Petén; Palenque and Yaxchilán in Chiapas; Comalcalco in Tabasco; Calakmul, Becán, and the communities of the Río Bec region of southern Campeche; Kojunlich and Tzibanché in southern Quintana Roo; Caracol, Lamanai, La Milpa, Xunantunich, Altun Há, and Lubaantún in Belize; and Copán in Honduras. Some of these cities did not become fully urban until the Late Classic period, after A.D. 600. Ongoing surveys and excavations are underway at many of these sites, and the history of their development is still being investigated. In the northern lowlands, most communities did not reach urban proportions until the Late or Terminal Classic periods (A.D. 600 to 1000); those that did include Edzná, in Campeche; Izamal, Dzibilchaltún, Chunchucmil, Ek Balám, Yaxuná, Xuenkal, and a host of smaller cities in Yucatán; and the megalopolis of Cobá in northern Quintana Roo.

Detailed settlement-pattern studies have been conducted at only a handful of these cities, though we are now starting to develop a general sense of their size. Most range from 3 to 10 square miles (8 to 26 square kilometers) in area, though a few of the larger sites for which we have survey data reached much larger proportions. Population estimates for most sites range

The heart of Tikal is the **Great Plaza,** once the setting for public celebrations and religious ceremonies. The **Great Plaza,** shown above and at right, covers more than two acres (one hectare), and is flanked by **Temples I** and **II** on the east and west, respectively; the steep-sided **Temple I** is shown above. The **Great Plaza** is bounded on the north side by the **North Acropolis,** a closely packed assemblage of temple-pyramids and lesser structures. The **Central Acropolis** anchors the plaza's south edge, and consists of a number of **Late Classic** structures, including the **Five-Story Palace.**

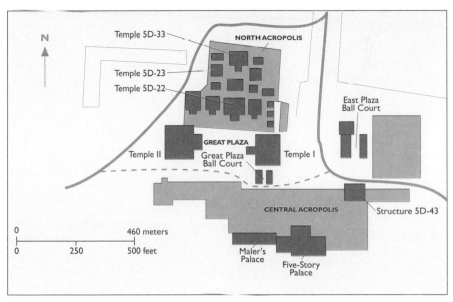

Pyramidal temples are a major feature of most Maya cities, and the well-explored, lowland site of Tikal, in Guatemala, has five. In this picture, Temple II stands in the foreground, while the roofcombs of Temples III and IV peer over the tropical vegetation. Temple IV, at right, is the tallest known Maya pyramid, rising 212 feet (67 meters) above its surroundings.

from 10,000 to 50,000 people; these figures apply to the Late Classic period (A.D. 600 to 900), when most Maya cities reached their largest size. The urban area of Cobá is estimated to have covered more than 25 square miles (64 square kilometers), with a population in excess of 50,000 people. Preliminary estimates made at Caracol indicate a site area of 34 square miles (88 square kilometers), and a population estimated at more than 100,000. Tikal, the most extensively surveyed city, had a 6-square-mile (16-square-kilometer) central core with several thousand buildings and an estimated population of 62,000. A densely inhabited rural periphery extends beyond the core over an area of 39 square miles (100 square kilometers), and likely supported an additional 30,000 people. Thus the total area of the site is estimated to have covered about 46 square miles (120 square kilometers), and to have supported a total population of some 92,000.

Most Maya cities have a central core with massive constructions set around large open plazas. It is the ruins of these monuments that have captured the modern public's imagination. They include large pyramidal temples, civic and religious buildings, and extensive residential complexes with palaces that housed the elites. The pyramidal temples are awe-inspiring; Temple IV at Tikal—the highest known—rises to 212 feet (67 meters). Four other pyramids at the site range in height from 140 to 190 feet (43 to 58 meters). The pyramids were built of cut limestone and rubble fill, with broad staircases leading to stone temples at the summit. The temples contain two or more rooms, with corbel-vaulted ceilings. Extending over the temples were large panels known as roofcombs, which were decorated with masks and religious motifs carved in stucco. Similar structures are found at many Maya sites. Excavations have revealed that many of these buildings were built on top of earlier pyramids, and often housed elaborate tombs of the cities' rulers.

Foreign visitors to the "downtown" area of a Classic Maya city would have encountered a dazzling display of sights, sounds, and activities that would have easily overwhelmed their senses. The temples and palaces were painted in a kaleidoscope of bright colors: red, green, blue, yellow, and black predominated. The plazas contained large monuments and sculptures, and the facades and interiors of temples were decorated with painted stone and stucco panels depicting religious motifs, deities, mythical figures, and dignitaries. Incense burned in the temples, where religious ceremonies were conducted, perhaps to the accompaniment of drums and trumpet music. Some of the plazas contained large, open markets, where a cornucopia of goods were available: basic foodstuffs, meats and vegetables, salt and condiments, medicinal herbs, pigments, stone and wooden tools and hunting weapons, obsidian blades, clothing, jewelry, dried fish, a menagerie of animals and exotic birds, jaguar skins, and possibly even slaves.

The great plazas that fronted the pyramids were the setting for public ceremonies in which religious rituals went hand-in-hand with celebrations of the historic events of the city's past. The achievements of past rulers were of paramount importance, as is indicated by the many stelae depicting rulers and members of the nobility, accompanied by hieroglyphic inscriptions commemorating major events in the lives of the royal families. Maya kings were believed to be the intermediaries between the people and the gods, and their complex rituals were designed to propitiate the deities and to ensure the well-being of their people; at their death, rulers also acquired divine status. The hieroglyphic texts contain dates of birth, marriage, accession to the throne, and the death and apotheosis of the rulers, as well as records of royal visits from rulers of other cities, interdynastic marriages, and conquests of rival cities.

The Great Plaza at Tikal is a monument to such past glories. Covering a total of more than two acres (one hectare), with a pyramid at each end, the plaza is flanked by two large acropoli, and contains 70 stelae and altars. At many cities, the acropoli contain a variety of buildings, including smaller temples, many public structures whose functions are not yet known, and extensive palaces that housed the rulers, their families, priests, scribes, and

The urban area of Cobá, in Yucatán, includes a number of satellite centers covering a total of more than 25 square miles (64 square kilometers). Linking them together is a network of *sacbés*, or causeways, as shown at right. The longest of these stretched west for some 62 miles (100 kilometers) from the Cobá capital to the satellite city of Yaxuná. The roadways consisted of a rubble core contained by vertical slabs, and were covered with a stucco surface.

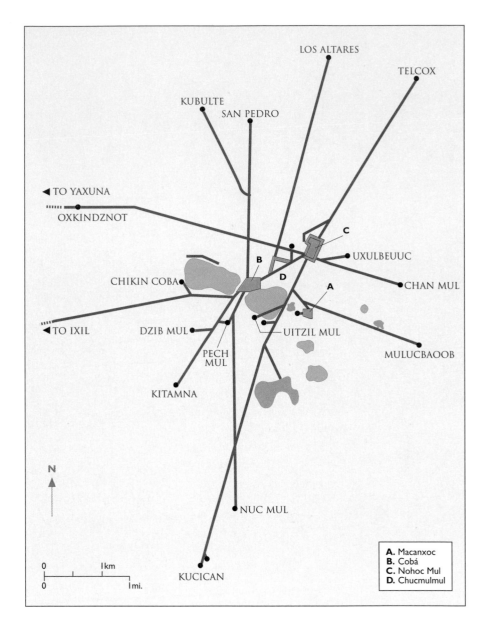

members of the lesser nobility. The palaces were arranged around internal courtyards, with restricted access, a repetitive pattern that was designed to ensure privacy for the elite.

Beyond the civic-ceremonial center lay the residential districts of the city, and the layout of these varies from site to site. These districts include a wide range of buildings, from courtyards with stone buildings and shrines—which housed the wealthier members of the community—to dispersed platforms that once supported perishable wattle-and-daub houses and kitchens

136

Cobá flourished during the Late Classic period, when around 50,000 people lived here. Recent findings indicate that Cobá continued to be an important city until about A.D. 1100, when, faced with the expansion of Chichén Itzá, the city was abandoned.

with thatched roofs. These latter structures often number in the thousands, and represent the residences of the common people—mostly laborers and farmers. At many sites, the houses are surrounded by walled-in yards, in which garden crops were grown. Maya cities that were distant from major sources of water had large artificial reservoirs—many of them former quarries and the source of much of the stone used in construction. Several cities, such as Tikal, Caracol, and Cobá, had extensive networks of sacbés connecting major monumental complexes and outlying satellite communities.

The latter were often in rich farming areas, and the sacbés provided a direct link between the city and its agricultural hinterland.

The cultural achievements of the Maya are legendary, and are reflected not only in their sophisticated urban planning and in their monumental architecture but in a myriad other areas as well. They manufactured some of the finest polychrome ceramics and clay figurines in the New World; exquisite lapidary work in jade and other exotic stones; beautiful sculpted stone monuments and wood carvings; leather goods; jewelry made from shell, obsidian, and other exotic materials; and a wide range of stone tools for use in the household, construction, farming, and hunting. The interiors of many temples, palaces and tombs were painted with murals depicting a variety of religious, mythical, and historical themes, often accompanied by inscriptions detailing the events. They had an advanced knowledge of mathematics, which included the use of zero and mind-boggling calculations of mythical events thousands of years into the past and future. They were also proficient astronomers, and centuries of celestial observations enabled them to develop a highly accurate solar calendar and to predict eclipses and the paths of many celestial bodies across the skies. Some of their buildings reflect this knowledge, and are aligned with solstices, equinoxes, and other astronomical events.

It is abundantly clear from the archaeological record that the Maya had evolved a highly stratified and complex society. At the pinnacle were the royal elite, whose dynastic lineages were closely entwined with the identity and history of each city. Below them were the nobility, the priests, scribes, bureaucrats, and warrior chiefs who looked after the affairs of the state. The next echelon was made up of master craftsmen, artists, traders, and others whose skills gave them a prominent social status. The lower social ranks were made up of craftsmen, laborers, farmers, and slaves, who constituted the majority of the population.

The growth of Maya cities was in large part the result of complex economic developments that went far beyond their original agricultural base. Research in the last three decades has revealed that many cities in the southern lowlands had highly developed systems of intensive agriculture. These included the use of tree-cropping, terraces, canals, and wetland farming that vastly increased their agricultural production, and enabled the Maya to support much larger urban populations. Craft production, feeding into regional and long-distance trade networks, also provided many cities with substantial wealth. A symbiotic system of exchange developed between various regions of the lowlands, and between the lowlands and the highland regions of the Maya area and the rest of Mesoamerica. Coastal products such as salt, fish, and shells were exchanged for inland agricultural staples and craft items, while lowland tropical goods—such as spices, cotton, ceramics, wood and leather items, exotic plumage, and pelts—were traded for highland mineral resources, such as jade, basalt, and obsidian. Much of this trade moved over water, along the coasts and up rivers, with bearers carrying it into the most remote corners of the inland forests.

The well-excavated site of Copán, in Honduras, is rich in carved stelae and glyphs. The majestic flight of steps on the large pyramid in the background is known as the Hieroglyphic Stairway, and contains the longest single Maya inscription ever discovered.

One of the most exciting areas of current research in Maya archaeology is that of Maya political organization. In recent years, major breakthroughs in the decipherment of Maya writing have enabled archaeologists to reconstruct the dynastic history of the rulers of several cities, and, while gaps remain, we now have records that stretch from the third to the ninth centuries A.D. The sequence of Tikal's 29 rulers, still not fully reconstructed, begins in the final years of the second century, and lasts until approximately A.D. 800. A complete list of rulers at Palenque runs from A.D. 396 to approximately A.D. 790, when the city went into decline. At Copán, a single monument known as Altar Q depicts all of the city's 16 rulers, whose reigns spanned several centuries, from approximately A.D. 435 to A.D. 820. Copán's 17th ruler acceded to the throne in A.D. 822, when the city was in its final years, and his fate is unknown. The last known monument erected by a Classic Maya ruler dates to A.D. 909, at Toniná, in Chiapas; by that time, most of the city-states of the southern lowlands had collapsed.

In keeping with the the Maya custom of recording their dynastic history in stone, the sides of Altar Q at Copán are carved with 16 seated figures—three of whom are shown here. These 16 individuals represent Copán's rulers, whose reigns spanned a period of nearly 400 years.

Closely related to the above research are attempts to define the size of Maya polities. The traditional view held that most Maya polities were small city-states whose domain encompassed the surrounding hinterland and a few secondary centers and villages.

One exception was the state of Cobá, which is conservatively estimated to have extended over more than 1000 square miles (2600 square kilometers) from the shores of the Caribbean to Yaxuná in central Yucatán. An important "skeletal" vestige of the state is a 60-mile-long (100-kilometer-long) sacbé connecting the latter city to the Cobá capital. Recent advances in epigraphic (hieroglyphic) research in the southern lowlands also suggest that several Maya polities were somewhat larger than originally envisioned. One of these was Dos Pilas, a Late Classic state that conquered several of its neighbors, including the city of Seibal, in the Pasión River drainage, during the eighth century, just prior to its own destruction. At its height, the Dos Pilas domain included 1500 square miles (3900 square kilometers) of territory. Tikal also evolved into a sizeable regional state during the Late Classic; its domain is now estimated to have covered 770 square miles (2000 square kilometers)—most of the north-eastern Petén—with an estimated population of 425,000.

Warfare and the conquest of increasingly large territories appear to have been prominent features of the Late Classic period, particularly in the last century before the collapse of Maya society in the southern lowlands. Many scholars believe that this activity was symptomatic of the factors underlying the demise of Classic culture. Growing populations, skirmishes over trade routes and their resources, environmental degradation due to deforestation and overfarming, and the resulting land shortages created an atmosphere of

A series of murals discovered in 1946 at the small site of Bonampak, in Chiapas, Mexico, shed new light on the nature of Maya political and military life. The reconstructed portion at right is a vivid portrayal of how the Maya dealt with war captives. In the lower section, warriors stand guard on either side of a doorway, while in the upper section the king and his court survey cowering prisoners awaiting sacrifice. The frieze in the top section represents the sky, and includes symbols for certain constellations.

fierce competition between the major regional states. In addition, the growing size of the noble class and their demands for ever-greater temples, palaces, and quantities of exotic luxury goods undoubtedly placed tremendous strains on the population as a whole. There is also some evidence to suggest that the rulers were losing their grip on society, and that infighting within the elites was on the increase, leading to the establishment of independent fiefdoms away from the capital. In sum, the rulers upon whom the Maya had depended for centuries failed to avert the growing crises that plagued the society, and the whole system unraveled. Beginning around A.D. 800, the population entered a drastic pattern of decline; one city after another was abandoned, and the tropical forest eventually reclaimed the great palaces and monuments. By A.D. 1000, all that remained were ruins.

The story of the Maya does not end here. New developments in the northern lowlands gave rise to a succession of city-states, which survived until the arrival of the Spanish in the 16th century. But that is another story. In any case, the achievements of the Classic period remained largely unknown until the 19th century, when scholars began to explore the remains of one of the ancient world's greatest civilizations.

The Chimú capital of Chan Chan stretches across the coastal desert of northern Peru. The adobe walls visible in this photograph delineate which may have been palace compounds. The city also contained administrative structures, thousands of storerooms, several water reservoirs,

the interiors of several rectangular enclosures, and massive burial platforms.

8

DESERT AND MOUNTAIN CITIES OF THE ANDES

The geography and ecology of the Andes are dramatically different from those of other regions of the world where early urban cultures developed. Here, in this mountainous region extending the length of South America's Pacific Coast, the first cities emerged in coastal desert or high mountain regions, and exploited a wide variety of environmental zones. The development of urbanism in the Andes was the outcome of a long process, evolving over several millennia, and, as in Mesoamerica, true cities

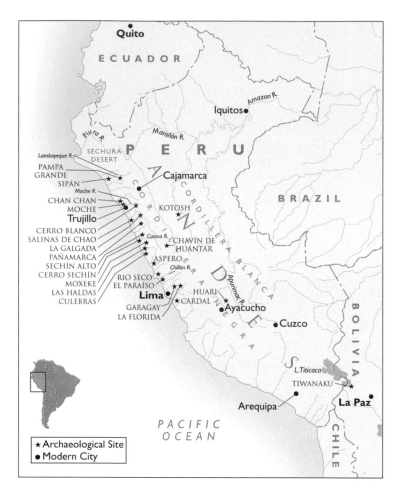

did not appear until relatively late—in this case, during the first centuries of the Christian era. While the two areas follow a roughly parallel and contemporaneous path of development, the cultures of the Andes were forged by quite different cultural, geographic, and economic factors.

One of the most marked differences between Andean and other early civilizations was the absence of a system of writing. Evidence of a script, a major building block in the development of state-level societies elsewhere, has never been found in Peru. The Andean peoples, like the Mesoamericans, also lacked wheeled vehicles, though they did have domesticated llamas and alpacas that served as beasts of burden. They were also skilled metallurgists, and produced the earliest and finest metal artifacts in the New World. Another unique feature of cultural evolution in the Andes was the important role played by the sea. The rich resources of the Pacific Ocean were a critical factor in the development of the earliest settled coastal communities. These resources lessened dependence on agriculture, which, in other parts of the world, figured prominently in the development of civilizations.

When the Spanish arrived in Peru in the 16th century, they encountered one of the New World's most sophisticated cultures, which was then dominated by the Inca Empire. This was a highly organized polity whose boundaries stretched from northern Ecuador to central Chile, and from the Pacific Coast to the upper reaches of the Amazon Basin. Simply put, it was one of the largest empires the world had ever seen. The Spaniards had little notion of the antiquity of the empire, or of the ruins of the earlier cultures that preceded it. Their primary interest lay in the vast treasures—mostly gold artifacts—that could be extracted from these ruins, and they embarked on a systematic campaign to excavate the palaces and elite tombs of the ancient Peruvian cities.

It was not until the early 19th century that travelers began to examine the vast remains of Peru's ancient cultures. One of the first to do so was the German Alexander von Humboldt, who in 1814 published the first account of Peruvian antiquities. He was followed by several distinguished scholars, including the Peruvian Mariano Eduardo de Rivero, the Swiss naturalist J.J. Diego de Tschudi, the Americans E.G. Squier and Adolph Bandelier, and the Germans

The early inhabitants of Peru adapted to a range of environments—from coastal desert to highland valleys and tropical forest. This "vertical mosaic" was a major building block in the development of complex societies. Proximity to the resources of the Pacific Ocean, for example, was a key factor in the appearance of the first coastal communities.

Alphons Stübel and Max Uhle who published extensive accounts, maps, and drawings of many of the ancient cities. Towards the end of the century, Max Uhle, with support from the University of California, carried out the first stratigraphic excavations at several sites along the coast of Peru, and developed a preliminary chronology of the pre-Inca cultures of the Andes. This chronology was further refined by Alfred Kroeber and his students in the 1920s and 1930s, and established the preeminence of the "Berkeley School," named for the institution that shaped much of the development of early Andean archaeology. Subsequent scholars from California, such as John Rowe, Dorothy Menzel, and Christopher Donnan, have continued this tradition.

A "Peruvian School" also developed in the early years of the 20th century, under the guidance of Julio Tello, a Harvard-educated scholar who became director of the National Museum of Peru and trained a whole generation of Peruvian archaeologists. Tello was the first to excavate Chavín de Huántar, where he identified the earliest complex society of the Andes, which he termed the "mother culture" of Peru. Following World War II, Andean archaeology came of age, and the number of scholars proliferated. In the last few decades, dozens of projects have been conducted by Peruvian, American, European, and Japanese archaeologists. The results of their work have revealed in more detail a gradual process of cultural development spanning several millennia, from the appearance of the first hunter-gatherers to the rise of the Inca Empire. These new projects have revealed a long sequence of complex pre-urban cultural development, with the appearance of large-scale early monumental architecture in the Preceramic and Initial periods (5000 B.C. to 800 B.C.), followed by the proto-urban Chavín Horizon (800 to 200 B.C.) and leading up to the first urban societies of the Early Intermediate period (200 B.C. to A.D. 600).

GEOGRAPHY AND ECOLOGY

One of the first items of information every tourist learns when he or she reaches Peru is that the country is divided into three ecological zones: the desert coast; the cordillera, or sierra (the Andean highlands); and the *montaña* and the *selva*, the forested eastern slopes of the Andes and the tropical forests of the Amazon lowlands, respectively.

The narrow desert coastal strip is interrupted at intervals by small river valleys. These rivers, which flow down from the Andes into the Pacific, form natural oases—the setting for early coastal farming societies. The rivers were eventually channeled into irrigation systems that drove the economy of many coastal cultures. The rich fisheries and abundant shellfish available along the coast provided an important additional source of sustenance for the human inhabitants. Because of this region's extreme aridity, these resources were particularly critical in the development of sedentary coastal communities: although the climate is moderate, with cool winters and warm summers, rainfall is almost nonexistent.

The German naturalist Alexander von Humboldt traveled extensively in Central and South America in the early 19th century, observing and classifying animals and plants and studying volcanoes, ocean currents, and climatic patterns. Humboldt's landmark accounts of Peruvian antiquities helped stimulate the first scholarly investigations of Peru's wealth of ancient remains.

Two large, parallel mountain chains, the western Cordillera Negra and the taller eastern Cordillera Blanca, form the north-south backbone of the highlands. In between these ranges are several large basins, whose fertile bottomlands provided a home for many highland cultures. In southern Peru, the ranges diverge, opening up a large, highland plain known as the *altiplano*, which stretches to Lake Titicaca and into western Bolivia and northern Chile. Rainfall in the highlands varies considerably, and increases with altitude. The larger highland valleys are well-watered, and many parts of the altiplano have lush grasslands, a rich source of fodder for grazing herds of llamas and alpacas. The climate ranges widely, from temperate in the valleys to freezing cold in the altiplano. The Andean peoples long ago adapted to the higher reaches of the altiplano, which rises up to 16,400 feet (5000 meters) in some areas.

To the east of the Cordillera Blanca lie the high cloud forests and lowland forests of the Amazon Basin. This was a marginal area in pre-Hispanic times, inhabited mostly by tribal groups who supplied the Andean societies with a variety of tropical forest products. It is an area of heavy rainfall, with a hot prevailing climate.

In the steep topography of the Andes, ecological zones change with every few thousand feet of altitude, leading to a varying range of adaptations that John Murra has termed a "vertical mosaic". In this scheme, inhabitants of the highland valleys and Andean slopes have, for millennia, exploited a diverse set of ecological niches. Depending on the season, a single community may farm corn and low-altitude crops in the lower parts of the valley, harvest potatoes and other tuber crops at higher altitudes, and graze their herds of llamas and alpacas in the higher reaches of the altiplano, which are unsuited for agriculture. This pattern of subsistence, coupled with the influx of farm products (mainly cotton and corn) and maritime products from the coast, has provided Andean peoples with a well-stocked larder, and buffered them in times of agricultural failure. This vertical mosaic has always been a key feature of Andean subsistence, and a major building block in the rise of complex societies.

EARLY COASTAL SETTLEMENTS

The oldest domesticated plants in the New World are represented by certain tubers, potatoes, gourds, beans, chili peppers, fruits, and fibers that were cultivated in some areas of the Andean highlands as early as 8000 B.C. However, these crops did not lead to an early village-farming way of life, but rather formed part of a seminomadic lifestyle, distinguished by hunting, gathering, and some cultivation, that lasted until relatively late—circa 2000 B.C. in most areas of the highlands.

The earliest permanently settled communities of the Andes appeared around 5000 B.C. in the coastal regions, and gave rise to a period known as the Coastal Preceramic, which lasted until 1800 B.C. Here, a culture known as the Fisherfolk developed an early reliance on the exploitation of marine resources.

Benefiting from the rainfall that occurs at high altitude in the Andes, farming settlements grew up in the fertile river valleys between the parallel ranges of the Andes Mountains. Highly adaptable Andean farmers still move seasonally from the lower regions, where they grow corn, to higher altitudes where hardier tuber crops such as potatoes flourish.

Their remains have been found at a few coastal sites in southern Peru and northern Chile, and consist of modest fishing hamlets made up of dome-shaped huts, built of cane supports covered with reed and grass thatch. The inhabitants made a living by harvesting fish and shellfish, and, to a lesser extent, by hunting and gathering. Their material culture included stone projectile points, nets, harpoons, and fishhooks made from cactus thorns, bone, and shell. The Fisherfolk also mummified their dead; the corpses of many individuals were carefully embalmed and dressed, and the skulls covered with clay masks with sculpted and painted facial details. Thus began an Andean cult of the dead that was to last until the arrival of the Spanish.

In most parts of the world, the transition to a sedentary way of life was made possible by farming, and was accompanied by the introduction of ceramics. In the Late Preceramic period of coastal Peru (3000 B.C. to 2000 B.C.), there were no ceramics, and farming ranked second in importance to the exploitation of marine and coastal resources. Nonetheless, University of Florida archaeologist Michael Moseley has argued that this highly unique maritime adaptation was the driving force behind the rise of complexity on the Peruvian coast. After 3000 B.C., the number and size of coastal settlements increased. The primary reliance on seafoods continued, but was increasingly supplemented by the cultivation of squash, gourds, and beans. Cotton was also cultivated, and textiles began to appear at many sites. Trade also flourished, as obsidian from the highlands and tropical products from the selva found their way to the coast, and marine shells were traded into the highlands. Eventually, a few very large communities with a pronounced degree of cultural complexity emerged. Most of

The largest of Peru's Preceramic sites is El Paraíso, located in the lower Chillón Valley. The site consists of nine stone complexes laid out in a U-shaped plan. This complex has been carefully restored to reveal a raised platform with a series of interconnected courts and rooms.

these settlements appeared on the central coast, and include El Paraíso, Rio Seco, Culebras, Aspero, Piedra Parada, and Salinas de Chao.

The largest Preceramic monument in the continent is found at El Paraíso, close to the mouth of the Chillón River, near Lima. This site, which covers 143 acres (58 hectares), consists of nine stone complexes laid out in a huge, U-shaped pattern. One of the complexes, which has been excavated and restored, consists of a raised platform with a series of interconnected courts and rooms. The main entry court, reached by two flights of stairs on the front of the platform, contains a square sunken patio with large fire dishes above each corner. Beyond the court is a large room with a bench in the rear, which may have been an altar. The adjoining rooms yielded few remains, and may have had either civic or residential functions.

PRECERAMIC COMMUNITIES OF THE HIGHLANDS

The advent of full-fledged agriculture, which included maize farming introduced from Mesoamerica, took place from around 2500 B.C. to 2000 B.C. in the highlands, and quickly spread to the coast after 2000 B.C. Llamas and alpacas were fully domesticated by 2500 B.C., and large-scale herding quickly spread throughout the upper reaches of the highlands.

The earliest sedentary communities in the highlands appeared around this time. Two of the most prominent were Kotosh and La Galgada, where early public architectural complexes have been dated to Late Preceramic times. Kotosh, located at an elevation of 6500 feet (2000 meters) on the central eastern slopes of the Andes, is dominated by two large artificial mounds, the larger of which reaches a height of 50 feet (14 meters). These mounds hold the remains of a series of superimposed temple chambers, surrounded by terraces and courtyards. The most impressive construction at the site is the Temple of the Crossed Hands, a large room with a sunken central court surrounded by walls with recessed niches. The north wall of this enclosure has a large central niche, and is flanked by two smaller niches, below which low-relief clay friezes depict crossed hands. In the center of the sunken patio floor was a stone-lined fire pit filled with ashes.

Similar structures have been found at La Galgada, located at an elevation of 3600 feet (1100 meters) on the western slopes of the central highlands. This site also has two large mounds, the largest of which stands 49 feet (15 meters) in height. Excavations of this mound have revealed a complex of ritual chambers, with niched walls and sunken courts with central fire pits. Temple chambers with sunken courts, fire pits, and niched walls are also found at early coastal centers such as Aspero and El Paraíso; this widespread pattern may reflect a shared set of religious practices throughout Preceramic Peru.

Beyond the obvious ceremonial nature of their monuments, very little is known about these early coastal and highland Preceramic settlements. Some of them clearly had large populations, while others show little evidence of residential remains, suggesting that the labor to build them was conscripted from nearby villages. Burials at these sites do evince a pronounced degree of social differentiation, clearly implying the emergence of an elite class that directed the construction of the monuments and supervised the ritual activities that took place in the sacred precincts. On the other hand, we know next to nothing about their social structure or political organization.

THE INITIAL PERIOD

The onset of the Initial Period (2000 B.C. to 800 B.C.) is characterized by the introduction of pottery and irrigation, and the spread of maize farming along the coast. Pottery vessels were useful for preparing and storing foodstuffs, and for brewing *chicha*, a beer made from corn. The growth in cotton farming and herding produced large surpluses of cotton and wool, while advances in loom weaving allowed for the mass production of cloth. The number and size of settlements throughout Peru grew dramatically during this period, driven in large part by the widespread exploitation of domesticated plants and animals, and by the continued exploitation of marine resources along the coast.

Continuing in the tradition forged in Preceramic times, the largest Initial Period settlements are found on the coast. Many share a similar U-shaped layout, with a *huaca*, or pyramidal mound, at the foot of a large, rectangular plaza

Excavations at the Late Preceramic site of Kotosh unearthed a series of temple chambers, seemingly built one atop the other by successive generations. One such construction is the Temple of the Crossed Hands, a well-preserved structure with a central court surrounded by walls that contain recessed niches. Beneath two of the niches are pairs of crossed hands modeled in clay, one of which appears here.

The pyramid complex of Sechín Alto, in Peru's Casma Valley, is one of the largest of the Initial Period's U-shaped sites. Dominating the site is the huge main pyramid, built of adobes faced with granite blocks and appearing in this aerial photograph as a large, light-colored square. A series of plazas, some with circular sunken courts, stretches away from the main pyramid to a distance of 4600 feet (1400 meters). At the time of its construction, this was the largest architectural complex in the Americas.

flanked by long platform mounds. The summits of the main mounds, which are reached by steep stairways from the plazas, contain complexes of courts and chambers dedicated to ritual activities. The most impressive of these is Sechín Alto, located in the Casma Valley. The U-shaped site is dominated by an enormous huaca that measures 820 by 984 feet (250 by 300 meters) at its base, and reaches a height of 144 feet (44 meters). The huaca is built of adobe bricks and faced with huge granite blocks, some of which weigh more than two tons. On its summit is a complex of courts and rooms. Extending 4600 feet (1400 meters) out from the mound are four rectangular plazas, three of which have large, sunken, circular courtyards. Surrounding the huaca and the plazas are several smaller mounds. The site is estimated to cover at least 740 acres (300 hectares); at the time of its construction in the middle of the second millennium, it was the largest architectural complex in the Americas. Other sites with monumental U-shaped ceremonial complexes are found at Cardal, in the Lurin Valley, La Florida and Garagay in the Rimac Valley, Las Haldas in the Casma Valley, and Huaca de los Reyes in the Moche Valley.

Only a few of these centers have been excavated. Still, limited excavations have revealed that the internal organization of the ceremonial centers can be quite complex. A reconstruction of the main group at Huaca de los Reyes has a main platform with an entry court, followed by a sunken patio surrounded by a series of temple chambers on its summit. Behind these, a staircase leads up to another, higher platform with a group of rooms on its summit. The lateral terraces also have entry courts with stairs leading up to shrines fronted by U-shaped entry courts. The plaza in front of the huaca is also flanked by platforms supporting entry courts leading into U-shaped structures. While little is known of the activities that took place in these complexes, it is most likely that they were primarily dedicated to rituals and administrative affairs. In some cases, they also celebrated military activities, as is evident at Cerro Sechín in the Casma Valley, where a series of stone relief monuments depict victorious warriors and mutilated captives. Evidence of warfare is also found in the highlands at several sites, where decapitated trophy heads are depicted on ceramic vessels. In some cases, the room complexes on the summits of the coastal huacas may have served as public storehouses. This was the conclusion reached by Thomas and Shelia Pozorski after excavating Huaca A at Moxeke, in the Casma Valley. Here, a large complex of rooms with niched walls surrounds an open courtyard; the entries to many of the rooms have high thresholds, a characteristic of storerooms in later times. The Pozorskis have suggested that the complex served as a depository for foodstuffs, ritual paraphernalia, and other materials.

As is the case with Preceramic sites, little is known about the residential sectors of these communities, whose remains are buried in the middens that surround the ceremonial complexes. Nonetheless, the architecture and material remains provide unmistakable evidence of an increasing degree of social complexity on a scale unmatched anywhere in the Western Hemisphere. However, despite their huge size, the settlements of the Initial Period are not true urban centers. While the large religious complexes do suggest a high degree of social organization, the sites do not exhibit the complex internal organization characteristic of cities, nor is there evidence of the social stratification or political organization that characterize fully developed state societies. On the other hand, the Pozorskis have suggested that the valleys of the central and north coasts were the home of several small polities, with regional capitals controlling

At the temple center of Cerro Sechín, in Peru's Casma Valley, an extraordinary series of carved stone panels, including this one featuring a club-wielding warrior, commemorates a bloody military victory.

The highland temple complex of Chavín de Huántar was to have far-reaching influence over architectural and artistic development in subsequent Andean societies. The site was first excavated by Julio Tello, who thought it represented Peru's earliest civilization. The temple complex was irrigated by runoff from the Cordillera Blanca. Shown here is the Old Temple, with a portion of the sunken circular plaza visible in the foreground.

groups of adjoining river valleys. This model would also apply to the highland areas, and it is likely that by 1000 B.C. many areas of the Andean region were under the control of small chiefdoms or proto-states.

THE EARLY HORIZON: CHAVÍN CULTURE

Towards the end of the Initial Period, around 900 B.C., a new center, Chavín de Huántar, emerged in the northern highlands. The Chavín culture flourished from 800 B.C. until around 200 B.C. The earliest architectural complex at the site, known as the Old Temple, consists of a large, U-shaped masonry building enclosing a sunken circular plaza. The overall dimensions of the structure measure approximately 245 by 405 feet (75 by 124 meters), and the different parts of the building range in height between 36 and 52 feet (11 to 16 meters).

The circular plaza, which was uncovered by the Peruvian archaeologist Luis Lumbreras in 1972, has a diameter of 69 feet (21 meters) and descends 8 feet (2.5 meters) below the surrounding courtyard. The walls are lined with flat stone slabs, sculpted with relief images of jaguars and of anthropomorphic figures bearing claws and fangs. One of the latter holds a club, or a staff of

A distinctive feature of Chavín architecture was the ornamentation of walls with detailed stone sculptures. Here, a large sculptured head projects from the upper portion of the walls of the Old Temple at Chavín de Huántar, in Peru. Within the Old Temple stands the fearsome stela known as the Lanzon (*below*), a lance-like 15-foot-tall (4.5-meter-tall) stone carved with the image of a fanged anthropomorphic deity. With its upper section set into the temple ceiling and its base embedded in the floor, it is thought to be the principal image of the Chavín cult.

authority, resembling a San Pedro cactus, which was a source of the mescaline used in hallucinogenic rituals throughout the Andes. Other hallucinogenic substances, such as snuffs and beverages imported from the Amazon jungle, were also common in Chavín rituals. Hallucinogenic use has been documented by drug-related paraphernalia recovered from excavations, including small, sculpted mortars (for grinding powders), bone trays, spatulas, miniature spoons, and snuff tubes, as well as sculptures depicting the San Pedro cactus.

The main building surrounding the circular plaza is honeycombed with a labyrinth of subterranean galleries, or passageways, in which were found ceramic vessels and sculptures depicting a wide range of mythical beings with jaguar, serpent, and cayman features. One of the most remarkable of these is the Lanzon, a stela carving in the shape of a human with jaguar fangs, and claws and hair in the form of serpents; this is believed to have been the Supreme Deity of Chavín de Huántar. Another major figure in the Chavín pantheon is the so-called "Staff God", an anthropomorphic figure depicted on a stela known as the Raimondi Stone. The Staff God has an elaborate radiating headdress, serpents for hair, canines and claws, and holds two vertical staffs made up of serpents.

Surrounding the main complex at Chavín de Huántar are the remains of an extensive settlement, which grew in size during the centuries following the building of the Old Temple. Richard Burger estimates that at its height, around 400 B.C., Chavín de Huántar covered approximately 100 acres (42 hectares), and had a population of 2000 to 3000 people. He suggests that the settlement was a proto-urban community, and the capital of a small regional polity, rather than that of a full state.

Chavín de Huántar appears to have been a major center of a religious cult that spread throughout Peru during the Early Horizon. Its distinctive style of architecture and the iconographic themes represented on its sculpture and pottery are found throughout the highlands and coastal valleys. In the coastal areas, these themes are widely represented on temple fronts, on textiles, and on pottery. The last included anthropomorphic and zoomorphic vessels with Chavín designs, often with stirrup spouts, a hallmark feature of Andean ceramic design that was to last for more than two millennia. The spread of this art style has been the focus of a debate that has spanned several decades. Was Chavín an early pan-Andean conquest state? Or was it a prominent cultic center, whose religious influence spread through trade? Given the limited evidence for warfare, most scholars would favor the latter interpretation. Nonetheless, many feel that the Chavín culture stood at the threshold of a new social and political order, and that the Early Horizon was a transitional period in which widespread social, religious, and economic interaction laid the foundations for later urban, state-level societies.

THE EARLY INTERMEDIATE PERIOD

From around 200 B.C. until A.D. 600, the Chavín culture was gradually replaced by several regional cultures that gave rise to the first state-level societies of the Andes. The most prominent of these were the kingdoms of the Moche on the north coast and the Tiwanaku in the southern highlands. The capitals of both kingdoms were fully developed urban centers; the Moche kingdom also had several regional capitals that may have also reached urban proportions.

After the Inca, the Moche are the best known of Peru's ancient cultures, mainly because of their ceramics, which are famous the world over for their exquisite craftsmanship. Moche ceramics, which come in a wide range of colors and are often decorated with stirrup spouts, were manufactured in myriad three-dimensional shapes. These include depictions of animals, plants, houses, deities, human figurines and head portraits, women giving birth, and humans engaging in a creative variety of sexual activities. Most of the stirrup-spout ceramics, which are known as libation vessels, were mold-made, and highly standardized. They also include some of the finest paintings executed on New World ceramics, exhibiting scenes of everyday activities, hunting, fishing, warfare, and ceremonial processions. The Moche are also widely known for the elaborate tombs of their rulers, priests, and warriors, which contain a rich array of artifacts, including the most exquisite items of native goldwork in the Americas. The rich tombs of the rulers of Sipán, recently uncovered by the Peruvian archaeologist Walter Alva, are a case in point, and have been the focus of much popular attention.

The capital of the kingdom was located at the site of Moche, in the valley of the same name along Peru's north coast. The main site features are two huge adobe pyramids, the Huaca de la Luna (Pyramid of the Moon) and the Huaca del Sol (Pyramid of the Sun). The latter, the largest pre-Hispanic construction in South America, originally measured 520 by 1100 feet (160 by 340 meters), and

One of the most exciting discoveries in Peruvian archaeology came in 1987 with the uncovering of the tombs of the Moche lords at Sipán. Accompanying the burials was a rich array of beautifully crafted artifacts, many of which are clearly visible at right. The ear ornament of gold and turquoise shown below was found in the same tomb, and is a perfectly detailed depiction of a warrior holding a war club and shield.

rises 135 feet (40 meters) in height. The structure was built entirely of adobe bricks—more than 100 million of them. In his excavations of the huaca, Michael Moseley discovered that it was constructed in segments, with the bricks from each section showing distinctive maker's marks; more than 100 such marks have been found, suggesting that they were manufactured by as many different communities, which also may have supplied the labor for constructing the edifice.

Much of our knowledge of Moche life in ancient Peru has been gleaned from the images portrayed in ceramics. The exquisite craftsmanship of Moche artisans is evident in this stirrup-spout vessel depicting a rugged and lifelike warrior's head.

Huaca del Sol (Pyramid of the Sun), located at Moche, capital of the Moche kingdom, is the largest pre-Hispanic structure in South America. The structure was built with more than 100 million adobe bricks. The bricks for each section bear the maker's mark. More than 100 of these marks, each representing a different community, have been found. This indicates that local communities contributed to the building of the edifice. The size of the huaca was drastically reduced in colonial times, when treasure hunters diverted the nearby Moche River to erode the pyramid.

The ability to marshal a labor force of this scale, undoubtedly numbering in the thousands, is a telling indication of the organizational capabilities and power of the Moche lords. Surrounding the huacas are the remains of a vast complex of administrative and ceremonial buildings, royal residences, courtyards, workshops, mausoleums, and cemeteries. At present, only part of the core of the settlement survives, covering some 250 acres (100 hectares). The site was originally much larger, but was devastated by floods in the sixth century, and sand dunes later covered over large parts of the city. The Spanish subsequently diverted the Moche River into the Huaca del Sol to mine it for its rich burials, and in the process wiped out the entire western part of the city.

Moche society was highly stratified, and its rulers sat at the top of a hierarchy of warriors, priests, bureaucrats, master craftsmen, traders, and artisans. The bulk of the population was made up of farmers, who worked large systems of irrigated fields, and fishermen, who plied the rich waters of the Pacific. Warfare was an important part of Moche life, as the many scenes in murals and on pottery indicate. These scenes include depictions of weapons and warriors, combat, and the sacrifice of prisoners. Much of this iconography is clearly a commemoration of military conquests.

As the population grew in their home valley, the Moche rulers launched a series of campaigns to conquer neighboring valleys, establishing control over their populations and rich agricultural systems. Their presence in these valleys was clearly indicated by fortified hilltop sites and by monumental administrative centers with Moche architecture and ceramics. Among the more prominent outposts are Sipán, in the Lambayeque Valley; Huancaco, in the Virú Valley; Pampa de los Incas, in the Santa Valley; and Pañamarca, in the Nepeña Valley. At this last

The upper-valley site of Pampa Grande in the northern Lambayeque Valley became the Moche capital circa A.D. 600. It replaced the former capital, which had suffered serious damage from El Niño floods. The focal point of the city was the great adobe mound known as Huaca Fortaleza, shown at right. Pampa Grande encompassed an area of 2.3 square miles (6 square kilometers), and contained residences of the elite, storage centers, and workshops for artisans and coppersmiths.

site, brilliantly colored murals commemorate the Moche conquest of the valley. At its height, the multivalley Moche state encompassed 15 river valleys along 350 miles (560 kilometers) of coastline, from the Piura Valley, near the Ecuadorian border, to the Huarmey Valley on the north-central coast. Their maritime presence extended all the way to the Chincha Islands on the south coast.

Shortly before A.D. 600, the Moche state began to decline. Moseley has noted evidence of massive flooding caused by the El Niño currents off the coast, which damaged the capital and several other river valley cities, and devastated the vital irrigation systems. At about that time, the capital was relocated to Pampa Grande, in the northern Lambayeque Valley, which then held sway over the northern river valleys, from Piura to Moche, for another century. Perhaps as a response to flooding, Pampa Grande was located far inland—some 30 miles (50 kilometers) from the sea. This city, which has been excavated by Izumi Shimada and his colleagues, covers an area of 2.3 square miles (6 square kilometers). It is dominated by a huge mound, known as the Huaca Fortaleza, which measures 900 by 590 feet (275 by 180 meters) at its base, and rises to a height of 180 feet (55 meters). Surrounding the mound is a densely concentrated mass of structures and courtyards, which include houses and related structures, complexes of storerooms, and workshops of artisans and coppersmiths. Several large rectangular enclosures served as administrative centers and residences of the elite.

Most of the Moche cities were abandoned around A.D. 700, for reasons that are not yet understood. There is a marked increase in the number of fortified hilltop settlements dating from the final century of Moche hegemony, raising the specter of political instability or even of highland military pressure. At the same time, there is evidence of continued flooding at several sites, which may have further weakened the agricultural base of the kingdom during its final years. Thus, the state's inability to recover may lie in both political and environmental processes that ultimately caused the social and economic systems to collapse.

THE TIWANAKU KINGDOM

On the high plains of the Bolivian altiplano, 9 miles (15 kilometers) south of Lake Titicaca, lies the city of Tiwanaku. Its location, at an altitude of 12,500 feet (3800 meters) above sea level, makes it the highest state capital of the ancient world. The site has been excavated since the 1930s, with most of the recent work carried out under the direction of the Bolivian archaeologist Carlos Ponce Sanginés, together with Alan Kolata, of the University of Chicago. Originally settled around 400 B.C., Tiwanaku gradually emerged as a major regional center during the early centuries of the first millennium. From approximately A.D. 375 to 700, it grew into the largest metropolis of the Andes, and its domain encompassed the Titicaca Basin of southern Peru and western Bolivia, to the coastal river valleys of southern Peru, and the high plains of northern Chile.

After A.D. 700, the state entered a period of gradual decline, and finally collapsed around A.D. 1000. Tiwanaku was the longest-lived of the Andean states, and it dominated the life of the southern Andes for almost a millennium.

The capital extends over an area of 1.5 square miles (4 square kilometers), and is estimated to have had a peak population of approximately 30,000 to 50,000 people. The most imposing structure of the city is the Akapana, a large, stepped pyramid faced with sandstone slabs, which measures some 650 feet (200 meters) to a side, and is 50 feet (15 meters) in height. On its summit are the remains of several stone buildings. Recent excavations by the Mexican archaeologist Linda Manzanilla have revealed that the rear of the Akapana contained a large sunken courtyard. Her excavations also exposed a complex, stone-lined drainage system and a series of offerings and human burials. Manzanilla believes that the structure was a ceremonial and priestly residential precinct dedicated to Viracocha, the Andean deity of creation.

To the north of the Akapana lies the Semi-Subterranean Temple, whose walls were decorated with huge, tenoned heads depicting human faces and skulls, possibly representing captives taken in warfare. Several stelae, including the Bennett Monolith, the largest known stela in the Andes, were once set into the floor of the plaza. The Bennett stela shows a relief depiction of an elaborately dressed individual, representing a ruler or a deity, holding a ceramic vessel in one hand and a staff of authority in the other.

Immediately to the west lies the Kalasasaya platform, reached by a broad staircase leading up to a monolithic gateway which gave access to the summit of the structure, where a statue known as the Ponce Monolith is surrounded by the remains of several rows of rooms. On the east side of the Kalasasaya lies a rectangular building known as the Putuni, believed to have been the palace of the rulers of Tiwanaku.

The ceremonial center of the Tiwanaku capital contained major public buildings, as well as the residences of the elite. Visible in this aerial photograph are the eroded remnants of the Akapana pyramid, at top right; the massive, square Kalasasaya platform, containing the Gateway of the Sun, in the center; the Semi-Subterranean Temple, with its sunken court, at the top; and the Putuni complex in the foreground.

The major buildings at Tiwanaku share a number of common features, the most prominent of which are sunken courtyards and the megalithic ceremonial gateways that provided access to the sacred precincts of the city. There are several of these, each carved from a single block of rock. The largest is the Gateway of the Sun, which has a complex, iconographic frieze carved in low relief above the doorway. The frieze shows a central figure with an elaborate headdress, often referred to as the Gateway God, standing on a three-tiered platform, holding two staffs of authority that end in condor heads. Flanking him are several winged figures, also carrying condor staffs. As numerous scholars have noted, the figure bears a strong resemblance to the Chavín Staff God, and may be the same deity.

The wealth of Tiwanaku was based on a complex agropastoral economy, supplemented by trade. Surrounding the capital is an extensive network of raised fields, which provided rich harvests of potatoes and other tuber crops. These fields, a major project of the Tiwanaku state, were managed by a hierarchy of communities under the control of the state capital. Flocks of llamas and alpacas provided beasts of burden, clothing, and meat. Colonies established by Tiwanaku

The entrance to the Kalasasaya bears a stark, monolithic gateway that frames the stela known as the Ponce Monolith. An enormous rectangular courtyard, the Kalasasaya may have served as a ceremonial precinct for rituals commemorating the ancestral rulers of the city.

at lower elevations to the east and west also provided the capital with warm-weather crops, such as maize, coca, and cotton, the last from the coastal valleys of the Pacific. Beyond those colonies under the direct political control of the capital, the elite of Tiwanaku obtained luxury goods through long-distance exchange networks. Llama caravans led by Tiwanaku merchants trekked across the southern Andean altiplano and into the high plains and coastal valleys of southern Peru and northern Chile, and may have reached northwest Argentina. Some of these trading expeditions traveled to communities as much as 500 miles (800 kilometers) away, and the round trip took several months. They carried textiles, ornately carved wooden and ceramic *keros* (beaker-shaped drinking vessels), snuff tubes and trays (for the ritual preparation and ingestion of hallucinogenic substances), and gold and copper objects. These were traded with local elites, who in turn supplied the merchants with regional goods for transport back to the capital. These included maize, coca, tubers, peanuts, squash, pumpkins, chili peppers, fruits, salt, minerals, basalt for making tools, tropical woods and nuts, tropical hallucinogens, the psychotropic San Pedro cactus, and shells from the Pacific Ocean.

The reasons behind the collapse of the Tiwanaku state are still not fully understood, although there is growing evidence that a prolonged drought may have been the critical factor. This drought, coupled with the salinization of the raised-field systems, would have dealt a major blow to the the economy of the Titicaca Basin, depleting the food supplies that sustained both the large human population and their herds of camelids. Eventually, the population of the basin began to shrink, and the city was abandoned, leaving behind only the monuments encountered by the Spanish in the 16th century.

The Gateway of the Sun is the largest of several megalithic ceremonial gateways at Tiwanaku. Flanked by winged attendants, the much-revered sun deity, often referred to as the Gateway God, is carefully carved into the lintel of this massive structure.

THE CONTINUING ANDEAN URBAN TRADITION

The preceding pages offer only a sketch of the emergence of the first cities and states of the Andes. This was only the beginning of a tradition of urbanism that was to develop further until the arrival of the Spanish. Following the decline of the kingdoms of the Moche and Tiwanaku, a new pan-Andean state developed in the highlands, with its large capital city at Huari, in the central highlands. This city had a population of 20,000 to 30,000, and held sway over a territory that extended throughout most of the north and central highlands and the adjoining coastal valleys from approximately A.D. 600 to 1000. The first true empire of the Andes—that of the Chimor—emerged shortly thereafter on the north coast of Peru, in the old homeland of the Moche. The Chimor Empire, the largest pre-Inca state in the Andes, extended along 620 miles (1000 kilometers) of coastline, from the Gulf of Guayaquil, in Ecuador, to the Chillón Valley, just north of Lima on the central coast. Its capital, Chan Chan, was the largest pre-Hispanic city in South America. Excavated by Michael Moseley and his students in the early 1970s, the city covers 2.3 square miles (6 square kilometers) on the shores of the Pacific in the Moche Valley, just a few miles away from the capital of the older Moche kingdom. Moseley estimates that Chan Chan had a population of 35,000 people, but it was only one of many large Chimú cities along the north coast, most of which have yet to be surveyed and excavated. Chimor was still growing when its expansion was cut short by the Inca, who conquered the capital around A.D. 1470 and incorporated its domain into their newer and much larger pan-Andean empire.

Historic mosques and more recent constructions punctuate the skyline of Cairo, the capital of Egypt, a city built upon the remains of rapid population growth and rural-urban migration fuel the expansion of such metropolises. In the ancient world, population increase

9

CONCLUSIONS

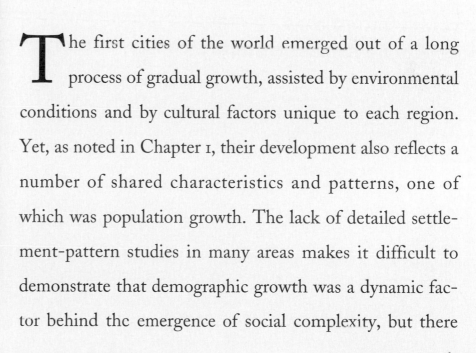

much older civilizations. Around the world, also contributed to the rise of the first cities.

The first cities of the world emerged out of a long process of gradual growth, assisted by environmental conditions and by cultural factors unique to each region. Yet, as noted in Chapter 1, their development also reflects a number of shared characteristics and patterns, one of which was population growth. The lack of detailed settlement-pattern studies in many areas makes it difficult to demonstrate that demographic growth was a dynamic factor behind the emergence of social complexity, but there is certainly enough general data to suggest that in all regions the total size and number of communities was on the increase just before the appearance of the first true urban centers. Moreover, the growth of communities was accompanied by increases in the volume and quality of craft goods produced, a clear indication that significant groups of the population were able to dedicate more time to activities other than farming, herding, or fishing. The emergence of groups of people who were no longer fully devoted to subsistence represented a major turning point in social development. Because there were now people who made a living in different ways, communities began to exhibit social differences. This first step towards the specialization of labor was, in many regions, the direct result of economic surpluses generated by improvements in the means of food production. The development of primitive irrigation or water-control systems in several areas is a good example, as is evident in Late Neolithic Mesopotamia, Predynastic Egypt, Lung-shan China, and Initial Period Peru. In Preceramic Peru, advances in fishing technology brought larger harvests from the sea, creating surpluses that allowed some people to make a living from other activities. The combination of population growth and improved technology—what systems analysts would refer to as a higher level of energy output—inevitably led to increased wealth and social diversity. In all the cultures we have discussed, the evidence for unequal access to resources and for increasing social differentiation is well documented in the periods preceding urbanization.

This shimmering hammered gold mask offers ample testimony to the skills of the Chimú smith who created it. As long ago as 200 B.C., metallurgy had become an advanced craft on Peru's north coast, and the flourishing of this and other crafts, particularly in the Moche and Chimú states, points to the existence of elite classes that no longer had to concern themselves with mere subsistence.

It appears that the interaction of population growth and advances in subsistence technology and craft production inevitably lead to urbanization, and thus represent a self-fulfilling prophecy. Yet these factors by themselves are not responsible for the emergence of the earliest cities. They may have been the basic building blocks, but other factors were also involved. A key factor was organization. In several early complex cultures, there is some evidence to suggest that the development of intensive subsistence technology and economic growth through craft production and trade contributed greatly to the emergence of political complexity, and that these developments were increasingly directed by elite groups who held sway over the other sectors of society. These elites, whose power lay in the management of such key areas as religion, intensive farming, or trade, worked together to establish a hierarchy that would perpetuate their control over society. It is now evident that the social composition and distribution of power within this hierarchy varied from culture to culture.

As noted in Chapter 1 and throughout this book, religious elites held prominent positions of power in every early urban society. These societies were heavily theocratic, and civic and religious authority merged at the top of the social pinnacle in the shape of the ruler, who in most instances held absolute power in both the civic and religious realms. The rulers of most early societies belonged to dynastic lineages that claimed descent from ancestral deities; for example, Egyptian pharaohs became gods in their lifetimes, while Maya rulers were elevated into the pantheon upon their death. Thus it is not difficult to see that centralized religion played an important organizational role in the development of early cities and states. This is particularly true in Egypt, in Mesopotamia, and among the early urban societies of the New World, where religion was central to all aspects of the culture.

The organization of secular activities was handled by other sectors of the elite, such as military leaders, merchants, engineers, and master craftsmen, and the available archaeological and historical evidence suggests that this is where the early societies begin to diverge. As Karl Wittfogel originally suggested, the development of large-scale irrigation systems directed by a class of water managers may have been a significant factor in the growth of some urban societies. This may have been the case in Mesopotamia, China, and in Tiwanaku and coastal Peru, but the evidence is not conclusive. Archaeologists have yet to demonstrate that complex, centrally controlled systems were in place before the advent of cities. On the other hand, there is little evidence to suggest that irrigation was a major organizational factor in the rise of urbanism in Mesoamerica, Egypt, and the Indus, even though irrigation systems were a prominent feature of those cultures.

In several early urban cultures, the role of large-scale craft specialization and trade appears to have been a critical factor in the growth of economic and social complexity. This was especially true in Mesopotamia, Egypt, the Indus, Teotihuacán, and the Andes, where craft production and long-distance trade were conspicuous features long before the full development of urbanism.

Other factors that are often linked to the evolution of early state societies are warfare and conquest, and there is little question that these played a prominent role in several of the societies discussed here. Such was the case in Predynastic Egypt, early Mesopotamia and China, in Formative Oaxaca, and in coastal Peru, where the power base of early city-states was consolidated through campaigns of conquest. The role of warfare in these societies is often commemorated in their art, which shows scenes of battle, captives, and weaponry. On the other hand, the evidence for warfare in the Indus region, in Formative Central Mexico, and among the Formative Maya is scant, though future research may alter the picture. The evidence for warfare in the early Andean highlands is also somewhat limited, although it appears to have been a central feature of later polities, such as those of the Huari and Inca.

Finally, as noted at the beginning of this book, the natural environment played an important role in the rise of complex societies. All early civilizations appeared in fertile or else potentially fertile regions, and the development of farming promoted population growth. The presence of domesticated animals gave certain regions an added advantage, not only in terms of sources of food and clothing but also as beasts of burden; this was the case in all of the Old World areas we have discussed, and in the Andes as well. The resources of the Pacific Ocean and the vertical mosaic of the Andes were important features in the rise of complexity in that region, as were lake resources in the development of Teotihuacán and Tiwanaku. All of the earliest cities in the Old World we have examined were located next to major navigable rivers. These were important sources of fish and water for irrigation, and also served as major avenues for trade. In similar fashion, rivers provided the lifeline for the early irrigation societies of coastal Peru.

The emergence of the earliest cities can thus be traced to a number of similar causes. However, the role that these played tends to vary from region to region, so that each culture displays its own highly distinctive pattern of development.

In examining the differences between cultures, one pattern that becomes immediately evident is the much earlier emergence of urbanism and state-level societies in the Old World. The earliest urban cultures of the Old World appeared between 3000 B.C. and 1500 B.C., whereas those of the New World did not emerge until the final centuries of the first millennium B.C. This is not surprising, given a longer history of human occupation of the Old World, and thus a longer time span for population densities to build up. This buildup spurred the earlier development of a broad agricultural base, which in turn encouraged further demographic growth. Also contributing to this pattern of growth was the availability of a wide range of potential animal domesticates, which formed an important part of the subsistence economy of Old World societies. Except for the dog and the turkey, Mesoamerica did not have any domesticated animals. The herding of camelids was important in the Andean highlands, but these animals were not as important as a food source as were, say, the sheep and goats of the Near East. Also, the role of animals in pulling wheeled transport was a critical technological innovation that was limited to the Old World. These and other technological advances had been adopted long before New World societies even began to exhibit signs of complexity.

In their attempt to explain the rise of urbanism in several parts of the world, past scholars often invoked the role of diffusion, suggesting that developments in one area had been the result of influences from another. Thus the rise of urban societies in Egypt and the Indus was based in part on Mesopotamian influences; in the New World, cultural advances in the Maya lowlands could be similarly traced to the Mesoamerican highlands. While there is evidence of interaction between these societies—mostly in the form of trade—there is little reason to suspect that either Mesopotamia or the Mesoamerican highlands had a significant role on the urban development of their neighbors. Each region we have discussed followed an independent or semi-independent trajectory towards social complexity, and the resulting cultures were so different that the role of diffusion can at best be considered minimal.

The distinctive nature of individual early urban cultures can be traced in part to the fact that they evolved to meet different needs. To begin with, they were shaped by local environmental conditions and by cultural responses to those conditions. Consider, for example, the differences in physical design between Old and New World cities. The cities in the Old World were located next to navigable rivers, and built around roads for wheeled traffic, whereas New World cities, many of which evolved in mountainous regions, were designed for pedestrian activities. Moreover, the driving organizational forces behind the growth of urban centers gave each culture a distinctive character. For example, many early urban centers developed a decidedly regal/ritual focus. This was particularly true of Egyptian cities, which grew out of concentrations of labor employed for the construction of royal monuments. Regal/ritual activities also permeated the early cities of the Maya lowlands and the Andes. The functions of other cities were heavily driven by economics: Sumerian cities were the nerve centers for growing hydraulic networks centralized around a temple economy while craft production

New York City is the archetype of our modern vision of the city, as both urban jungle and the dynamic focus of cultural, economic, political, and social life. Archaeological research into the growth of the world's first cities is providing us with insights into the fragile and complex balance that sustains urban life today.

and trade were major factors in Mesopotamia, Teotihuacán, and the Harappan cities. Early cities and states served and were driven by varying combinations of economic and ideological functions, and as long as the elites were able to maintain credibility for these functions by meeting the needs and expectations of their inhabitants, the cities thrived. When the states no longer met these needs, their systems lost their vitality and viability, and their cities collapsed (or else were conquered by other states).

Archaeological research into the emergence of cities has come a long way in the last few decades, yielding both a chronological framework for the prehistoric development of urbanism and a general understanding of the major factors that gave rise to cities. It has also provided some tentative ideas on why some of the earliest cities deteriorated and collapsed. While archaeologists have much to learn about urban collapse, their findings to date clearly indicate that cities have always been complex and fragile systems in constant need of dynamic leadership that can respond to crisis and provide the economic and cultural renewal so crucial to a city's survival. This is probably the most important lesson the past holds for the cities of the present and future.

REFERENCES

CHAPTER 1

In this chapter, I have presented a highly simplified sketch of some of the central theoretical issues involved in the rise of urbanism and state-level societies. More involved discussions can be found in the works by Blanton, Haas, Service and Redman, and in the collection of essays edited by Cohen and Service. Childe's article, a classic in the field, has also been reprinted in several collections of papers on ancient cities. Another classic work is Adams' comparative study of the rise of urbanism in Mesopotamia and Mesoamerica. The general literature on the growth of urbanism around the world is quite extensive; the reader wishing to embark on such a journey will find excellent points of departure in the studies by Mumford and Sjoberg, and in the volume edited by Davis.

ADAMS, R.M. 1966 *The Evolution of Urban Society*. Aldine Publishing Company, Chicago.

BLANTON, R.E. 1976 Anthropological Studies of Cities. *Annual Review of Anthropology*, 5: 249-64.

CHILDE, V.G. 1950 The Urban Revolution. *Town Planning Review*, 21: 3-17.

COHEN, R., AND E.R. SERVICE (EDITORS) 1978 *Origins of the State. The Anthropology of Political Evolution*. Institute for the Study of Human Issues, Philadelphia.

DAVIS, K. (EDITOR) 1973 *Cities: Their Origin, Growth and Human Impact. Readings from Scientific American*. W.H. Freeman and Company, San Francisco.

HAAS, J. 1982 *The Evolution of the Prehistoric State*. Columbia University Press, New York.

MUMFORD, L. 1961 *The City in History: Its Origins, Its Transformations, and Its Prospects*. Harcourt Brace & World, Inc., New York.

REDMAN, C.L. 1978 *The Rise of Civilization. From Early Farmers to Urban Society in the Ancient Near East*. W.H. Freeman and Company, San Francisco.

SERVICE, E.R. 1975 *Origins of the State and Civilization*. W.W. Norton & Co. Inc., New York.

SJOBERG, G. 1960 *The Preindustrial City Past and Present*. The Free Press, New York.

CHAPTER 2

Whitehouse's book contains a general account of the earliest cities of the Near East. More detailed overviews of the development of complex society are available in the works by Lloyd, Maisels, Nissen, and Redman. Kramer has written the classic account of Sumerian society and culture; a more up-to-date work is that of Crawford. Pollock's article offers an excellent in-depth overview of current research on the period when the first cities emerged. Fagan's work is a detailed history of archaeological research in Mesopotamia.

CRAWFORD, H. 1991 *Sumer and the Sumerians*. Cambridge University Press, Cambridge.

FAGAN, B.M. 1979 *Return to Babylon*. Little, Brown & Company, Boston.

KRAMER, S.N. 1967 *The Sumerians*. The University of Chicago Press, Chicago.

LLOYD, S. 1978 *The Archaeology of Mesopotamia. From the Old Stone Age to the Persian Conquest*. Thames and Hudson, London.

MAISELS, C.K. 1990 *The Emergence of Civilization. From Hunting and Gathering to Agriculture, Cities, and the State in the Near East*. Routledge, New York.

NISSEN, H.J. 1988 *The Early History of the Ancient Near East 9000-2000 B.C.* University of Chicago Press, Chicago.

POLLOCK, S. 1992 Bureaucrats and Managers, Peasants and Pastoralists, Imperialists and Traders: Research on the Uruk and Jemdt Nasr Periods in Mesopotamia. *Journal of World Prehistory*, 6 (3): 297-336.

REDMAN, C.L. 1978 *The Rise of Civilization. From Early Farmers to Urban Society in the Ancient Near East*. W.H. Freeman & Company, San Francisco.

WHITEHOUSE, R. 1977 *The First Cities*. Phaidon, Oxford; E.P. Dutton, New York.

CHAPTER 3

The literature on ancient Egypt is almost endless, and coming up with a selected list is no easy task. Four very readable accounts are those of Aldred, David, Hoffman, James, and Trigger. Kemp's study is a more sophisticated and up-to-date text, with excellent illustrations. The collection by Trigger and others contains a series of essays on changing Egyptian society from the Predynastic period to Alexandrian times, written by leading scholars. The recent articles by Hassan and Wenke present thoughtful overviews of current research. Fagan has written an excellent and entertaining history of Egyptology.

ALDRED, C. 1986 *The Egyptians*. 2nd edition. Thames and Hudson, London and New York.

DAVID, A.R. 1988 *The Egyptian Kingdoms*. Phaidon Press, Oxford; E.P. Dutton & Co., New York.

HASSAN, F.A. 1988 The Predynastic of Egypt. *Journal of World Prehistory*, 2(2): 135-85.

FAGAN, B.M. 1975 *The Rape of the Nile*. Charles Scribner's Sons, New York.

HOFFMAN, M.A., 1979 *Egypt Before the Pharaohs*. Alfred A. Knopf, New York.

JAMES, T.G.H. 1988 *Ancient Egypt: The Land and its Legacy*. University of Texas Press, Austin.

KEMP, B.J. 1989 *Ancient Egypt: Anatomy of a Civilization*. Routledge, London and New York.

TRIGGER, B.G. 1993 *Ancient Egypt as an Early Civilization*. American University in Cairo, Cairo.

TRIGGER, B.G., B.J. KEMP, D. O'CONNOR, AND A.B. LLOYD 1983 *Ancient Egypt. A Social History*. Cambridge University Press, Cambridge.

WENKE, R.J. 1991 The Evolution of Early Egyptian Civilization: Issues and Evidence. *Journal of World Prehistory*, 5 (3): 279-329.

CHAPTER 4

Readers can trace the history of research on Harappan civilization in the collection of landmark articles edited by Possehl. A comprehensive account of the archaeology of the Indus culture can be found in the work by the Allchins. Fairservis has written an extensive study on the decipherment of the Indus script. The articles by Fairservis, Kenoyer, and Possehl all present excellent overviews of recent research in the Indus region, with markedly different perspectives on the causes behind the rise of urbanism.

ALLCHIN, B., AND R. ALLCHIN 1982 *The Rise of Civilization in India and Pakistan*. Cambridge University Press, Cambridge and New York.

FAIRSERVIS, W.A. 1989 An Epigenetic View of the Harrapan Culture in *Archaeological Thought in America*, ed. C.C. Lamberg-Karlovsky, pp. 205-17. Cambridge University Press, Cambridge.
1992 *The Harrapan Civilization And Its Writing. A Model for the Decipherment of the Indus Script*. E.J. Brill, Leiden.

KENOYER, J.M. 1991 The Indus Valley Tradition of Pakistan and West India. *Journal of World Prehistory*, 5 (4): 331-85.

POSSEHL, G.L. (EDITOR) 1979 *Ancient Cities of the Indus*. Carolina Academic Press, Durham.

1990 Revolution in the Urban Revolution: The Emergence of Indus Urbanization. *Annual Review of Anthropology*, 19: 261-82.

CHAPTER 5

The works of Kwang-chih Chang are the main sources in English on ancient China. His monumental synthesis of the prehistory of China, now in its fourth edition, is the most widely consulted text on the subject. Chang has also written a detailed account of Shang civilization, which is the best source on the rise of civilization; his reconstruction of the period is based on a large body of archaeological data, as well as extensive historical records. He has also edited a collection of papers by leading scholars on recent developments in Shang archaeology. Two other excellent sources are the collection of authoritative papers edited by Keightley, and Wheatley's in-depth study of ancient Chinese cities.

CHANG, K.C. 1980 *Shang Civilization*. Yale University Press, New Haven.

CHANG, K.C. (EDITOR) 1986 *Studies of Shang Archaeology*. Yale University Press, New Haven.

CHANG, K.C. 1986 *The Archaeology of Ancient China*. 4th edition. Yale University Press, New Haven.

KEIGHTLEY, D.N. (EDITOR) 1983 *The Origins of Chinese Civilization*. University of California Press, Berkeley.

WHEATLEY, P. 1971 *The Pivot of the Four Quarters; A Preliminary Enquiry into the Origins and Character of the Ancient Chinese City*. Aldine Publishing Company, Chicago.

CHAPTER 6

Weaver's text is the most widely used general source on the archaeology of Mesoamerica; the texts by Adams and Coe also offer up-to-date surveys of the subject. Sabloff has written an informative introduction to pre-Hispanic Mexican urbanism. For recent research on the Olmec horizon in Mesoamerica, the reader may consult the collection of papers edited by Sharer and Grove, and the recent overview by Grove. Whitecotton offers a general account of Zapotec culture; a more technical and current collection of papers can be found in the volume of papers edited by Flannery and Marcus. An excellent collection of essays on recent research at Teotihuacán is available in the volume edited by Berlo.

ADAMS, R.E.W. 1991 *Prehistoric Mesoamerica*. University of Oklahoma Press, Norman.

BERLO, J.C. (EDITOR) 1992 *Art, Ideology, and the City of Teotihuacan*. Dumbarton Oaks, Washington, D.C.

COE, M.D. 1994 *Mexico. From the Olmecs to the Aztecs*. 4th edition. Thames and Hudson, London and New York.

FLANNERY, K.V., AND J. MARCUS (EDITORS) 1983 *The Cloud People: Divergent Evolution of the Zapotec and Mixtec Civilizations*. Academic Press, New York.

GROVE, D.C. 1992 The Olmec Legacy. *Research & Exploration*, 8 (2): 148-65. National Geographic Society, Washington, D.C.

SABLOFF, J.A. 1989 *The Cities of Ancient Mexico. Reconstructing a Lost World*. Thames and Hudson, London and New York.

SHARER, R.J., AND D.C. GROVE (EDITORS) 1990 *Regional Perspectives on the Olmec*. Cambridge University Press, Cambridge.

WHITECOTTON, J.W. 1977 *The Zapotecs. Princes, Priests, and Peasants*. University of Oklahoma Press, Norman.

WEAVER, M.P. 1993 *The Aztecs, Maya and their Predecessors. The Archaeology of Mesoamerica*. 3rd Edition. Academic Press, San Diego.

CHAPTER 7

Two excellent popular introductions to the ancient Maya can be found in Culbert, and Stuart and Stuart. A more involved account is available in Schele and Freidel. There are several informative texts on the subject, including those of Coe; Morley, Brainerd, and Sharer; and Sabloff. Coe has written a detailed account of the history of research on ancient Maya hieroglyphic writing, and Culbert has edited a collection of papers summarizing the most recent advances in the study of Classic Maya political history.

COE, M.D. 1992 *Breaking the Maya Code*. Thames and Hudson, London.

1993 *The Maya*. 5th edition. Thames and Hudson, London.

CULBERT, T.P. (EDITOR) 1991 *Classic Maya Political History. Hieroglyphic and Archaeological Evidence*. Cambridge University Press, Cambridge.

1993 *Maya Civilization*. St. Remy Press, Montreal; Smithsonian Books, Washington, D.C.

MORLEY, S.G., G.W. BRAINERD, AND R.J. SHARER 1994 *The Ancient Maya*. 5th edition. Stanford University Press, Stanford.

SABLOFF, J.A. 1990 *The New Archaeology and the Ancient Maya*. Scientific American Library, New York.

SCHELE, L., AND D.A. FREIDEL 1990 *A Forest of Kings. The Untold Story of the Ancient Maya*. William Morrow and Company, Inc., New York.

STUART, G., AND G. STUART 1993 *Lost Kingdoms of the Maya*. National Geographic Society, Washington, D.C.

CHAPTER 8

Three excellent recent overviews of Andean archaeology are available in the texts by Moseley and Richardson, and in the collection of papers edited by Keatinge. The older text by Lumbreras is also informative and well illustrated. Moseley has highlighted the role of coastal resources in his study of the maritime foundations of Andean civilization. The volume edited by Haas, Pozorski, and Pozorski contains several detailed studies of the origins of state-level societies in the Andean region. Comprehensive in-depth treatment of regional cultures are available in the works by Benson on the Moche, Burger on Chavín, and Kolata on Tiwanaku.

BENSON, E.P. 1972 *The Mochica: A Culture of Peru*. Praeger Publishers, New York.

BURGER, R.L. 1992 *Chavín and the Origins of Andean Civilization*. Thames and Hudson, London.

HAAS, J.S., S. POZORSKI, AND T. POZORSKI (EDITORS) 1987 *The Origins and Development of the Andean State*. Cambridge University Press, Cambridge and New York.

KEATINGE, R.W. (EDITOR) 1988 *Peruvian Prehistory. An Overview of Pre-Inca and Inca Society*. Cambridge University Press, Cambridge.

KOLATA, A.L. 1993 *The Tiwanaku: Portrait of an Andean Civilization*. Blackwell, Cambridge, MA, and Oxford.

LUMBRERAS, L.G. 1974 *The Peoples and Cultures of Ancient Peru*. Smithsonian Institution Press, Washington, D.C.

MOSELEY, M.E. 1975 *The Maritime Foundations of Andean Civilization*. Cummings Publishing Company, Menlo Park, California.

1992 *The Incas and their Ancestors. The Archaeology of Peru*. Thames and Hudson, London.

RICHARDSON, J.B. III 1994 *People of the Andes*. St. Remy Press, Montreal; Smithsonian Books, Washington, D.C.

CHAPTER 9

As in Chapter 1, I have only barely touched on some of the salient issues surrounding the rise of urbanism. For lengthier treatments, the reader should consult the books listed for Chapter 1.

INDEX

PICTURE CREDITS

Front cover photograph by Steve Vidler/Comstock
Back cover photograph by Victor R. Boswell, Jr./National Geographic Society

8,9 Victor R. Boswell, Jr./National Geographic Society
10 Gordon R. Willey
11 from Bruce Trigger, *Gordon Childe* (1980)
13 Victor R. Boswell, Jr./National Geographic Society
14 Buddy Mays
16,17 Nik Wheeler
20,21 Buddy Mays
21 *(right)* Dan Porges/Peter Arnold, Inc.
22,23 Robert Frerck/Odyssey
25 Jonathan Wright/Photographers/Aspen
28 George Gerster/Comstock
29 Nik Wheeler
30,31 *(both)* Robert Frerck/Odyssey
33 Victor R. Boswell, Jr./National Geographic Society
36,37 Nik Wheeler
39 Nik Wheeler
40,41 *(all)* The Bettmann Archive
42 The Bettmann Archive
43 The Ashmolean Museum, Oxford
44,45 Werner Forman/Art Resource
46 The Ashmolean Museum, Oxford
47 Werner Forman/Art Resource
51 Nik Wheeler
52 E. Otto/Comstock
53 Yann Arthus-Bertrand/Altitude/Peter Arnold, Inc.
54 Larry Fisher/Masterfile
55 Robert Azzi/ Woodfin Camp & Associates
58,59 Dilip Mehta/Woodfin Camp & Associates
61,63 *(both)* Dilip Mehta/Woodfin Camp & Associates
64 The Mansell Collection
66,67 Dilip Mehta/Woodfin Camp & Associates
67 *(right)* from Sir Mortimer Wheeler, *The Indus Civilization*, (1968)
68 Dilip Mehta/Woodfin Camp & Associates
69 *(upper)* Robert Hardin/ Peter Arnold, Inc.
69 *(lower)* The Mansell Collection

70,71 Will Williams/Wood Ronsaville Harlin, Inc.
73 The Mansell Collection
78,79 Dennis Cox/China Stock
80 *(both)* The Bettmann Archive
83 Wolfgang Kaehler
84,85 Karen Barnes/Wood Ronsaville Harlin, Inc.
87 The Royal Ontario Museum
88 Courtesy of The Freer Gallery of Art
89 The Royal Ontario Museum
91 Courtesy of The Freer Gallery of Art
92 The Royal Ontario Museum
93,95 *(both)* Courtesy of The Freer Gallery of Art
98,99 Steve Vidler/Comstock
103 *(left)* Kenneth Garrett
103 *(right)* Kevin Schafer
104 Nik Wheeler
105 from Jeremy Sabloff, *The Cities of Ancient Mexico* (1989)
106,107 Andrew Rakocky/Bruce Coleman, Inc.
109 *(left)* Kevin Schafer
109 *(right)* Robert Frerck/Odyssey
110 Kevin Schafer
112 Steve Vidler/Comstock
113 from Jeremy Sabloff, *The Cities of Ancient Mexico* (1989)
114 Robert & Linda Mitchell
115 The Art Institute of Chicago
120,121 Kenneth Garrett
123 Dagli Orti
127 Courtesy of Will Andrews, Middle American Research Center, Tulane University
128,129 Courtesy of Bruce Dahlin, Howard University
129 *(lower)* Dave Houser
131 David Freidel
133 Ken Laffal
134 Kevin Schafer
137 Martha Cooper/Peter Arnold, Inc.
139,140 *(both)* Kenneth Garrett
141 The Peabody Museum/Harvard University, Illustration by Hillel Burger

142,143 Dave Houser
145 The Bettmann Archive
147 Robert Frerck/The Stock Market
148 James B. Richardson III
149 from Izumi and Sono, *Excavations at Kotosh*, (1963)
150 Servicio Aerofotográfico Nacional, Peru
151 James B. Richardson III
152 Ric Ergenbright
153,154 *(both)* Ric Ergenbright
155 *(left)* James B. Richardson III
155 *(right)* Christopher Donnan
156 *(upper)* The Art Institute of Chicago
156,157 *(both)* James B. Richardson III
159 Marilyn Bridges
160 Fernando Sánchez
161 Wolfgang Kaehler
162,163 Buddy Mays
164 Robert Frerck/Odyssey
167 Larry Fisher/Masterfile
176 Barbara Andrews

AUTHOR'S ACKNOWLEDGMENTS

I undertook the writing of this book at the invitation of the series editor, Jerry Sabloff. I was at first reluctant to take on the project, given my lack of firsthand familiarity with the ancient cities of the Old World, but his encouragement and constant editorial advice greatly eased the task. Another major source of support came from my wife, Mary Andrews, who carefully edited each chapter, curtailing my propensity for clichés and technical jargon, a task the reader will no doubt appreciate.

Over the years, numerous people have educated me on the issues surrounding the archaeological investigation of ancient cities, and I would like to thank them all; they include, among others, Will Andrews, Antonio Benavides, Arlen and Diane Chase, Pat Culbert, David Freidel, Tomás Gallareta, Ed Kurjack, Gary McDonogh, Andrew Moore, Michael Moseley, David Pendergast, Bill Rathje, Fernando Robles, and Jerry Sabloff. This project involved a great deal of library work, and I relied extensively on the services of Holly Barone, the Inter-Library Loan librarian at the New College/USF Library, to acquire many of the source materials.

Finally, I would like to thank Carolyn Jackson, Alfred LeMaitre, Philippe Arnoldi, Geneviève Monette, Olga Dzatko, Jennifer Meltzer, and the other members of the St. Remy Press staff who oversaw the production of this book. It was a pleasure working with such a friendly and professional group. I am also indebted to the various institutions and scholars who kindly provided the illustrations for this book.

Anthony P. Andrews
Sarasota, Florida